THE Paper Boomerang Book

THE Paper Boomerang Book

Build Them, Throw Them, and Get Them to Return Every Time

Mark Latno

CHICAGO REVIEW PRESS

Library of Congress Cataloging-in-Publication Data
Latno, Mark.
    The paper boomerang book : build them, throw them, and get them to return every time / Mark Latno.
        p. cm.
    Includes bibliographical references.
    ISBN 978-1-56976-282-0
1. Paper work—Juvenile literature. 2. Boomerangs—Juvenile literature. I. Title.

TT870.L32 2010
745.54—dc22

                                                    2010007251

Cover design and cover illustrations: Andrew Brozyna, AJB Design, Inc.
Interior design: Scott Rattray
All interior images from the author's collection unless otherwise noted.

© 2010 by Mark Latno
Published by Chicago Review Press, Incorporated
814 North Franklin Street
Chicago, Illinois 60610
ISBN 978-1-56976-282-0
Printed in the United States of America
5 4 3 2 1

To the elementary school students in the Los Angeles Unified School District,
who have inspired me with their warmhearted smiles and other small kindnesses.

Contents

Introduction

Since the dawn of civilization, men and women have been hurling things through the air. But no other projectile they have ever fashioned and thrown displays such odd and fascinating behavior as the returning boomerang. Just as rainbows, bubbles, and waves are apt to inspire a sense of joy, wonder, and fascination, so it is with boomerangs. And although the boomerang is perhaps just as strange and beautiful as these other simple things, since it is a solid object, it is easier to hold in one's hands, manipulate, and study.

This book will teach you how to make paper boomerangs quickly; how to alter them to fly in large spaces, such as auditoriums, or in smaller rooms, such as bedrooms, living rooms, or classrooms; and how to decorate them in a variety of ways. *The Paper Boomerang Book* is for students, parents, and teachers, and anyone who has ever been curious about boomerangs and wished to have a little fun with them. The basic method of construction and basic throwing techniques are set forth in easy-to-understand photographic illustrations. You will find that the paper boomerangs in this book are a cinch to make, graceful in flight, and fun to fly.

In 1963, when Americans scientists were developing the space program and pushing the study of aerodynamics with the flights of the X-15, I saw a television program in which a professor of aeronautics flew a small four-bladed boomerang. It was about eight inches in length. He only threw it twice, hardly moving his arm, but each time it zipped around in a perfect, tight little circle. He caught it so effortlessly both times that it seemed almost magical.

I was hooked. If he could do it, so could I. I went down to the garage and cut out two 20-by-2-inch wings out of ¼-inch plywood. I crossed the wings, nailed them together, and bent the nails over on the backside with a hammer. I filed the front surfaces to make an airfoil. Then I took this crude flyer up to the grassy hill at the local high school. I threw it. It went straight out as if it would end up on the next block, but at the last second it curved upward and came hurtling back. It was far too big and heavy to catch, so I stood aside and let it land a couple feet from me. I experimented with these heavy boomerangs for about a year. (Once, something momentarily distracted me as one was returning. I looked away, and the boomerang clobbered me, nearly knocking me over.)

More than 30 years later, I began experimenting with small paper boomerangs in the classroom. These little paper flyers worked amazingly well. Many of my students suggested that I write a book on the subject, so I pulled out my old math and physics texts and started doing formal experiments with different types of paper. I studied the physics of flight to improve these boomerangs' flying abilities, and then started giving throwing lessons to my students. Eventually, I became so good at making and flying paper boomerangs that I could zip them around the room and get them to land on my desk or in my lap. My students and I have had a great deal of fun with these simple boomerangs.

While you're reading through this book, do not let the chapter on theory scare you. It is truly easy to make, throw, and fine-tune paper boomerangs. Even very young children can be taught to throw them. One of the most enjoyable experiences I have ever had as a teacher was giving boomerang-throwing lessons to preschool students. I selected a little girl and taught her how to throw one. She wound up her arm and hurled the boomerang for the first time—with perfect natural technique! But she lost sight of it and just stood there wondering where it went. When it came around in a perfect circular path and bopped her in the back of her head, a little wave of laughter spontaneously washed over the room.

Making paper boomerangs is an art that anyone can learn, and everything you need to know to be successful is in this book.

1

A Brief History of Boomerangs

Origins

The exodus of modern man, *Homo sapiens sapiens*, from Africa is now thought to have taken place around 90,000 years ago. For about 20 percent of that time—approximately 20,000 years—humans probably have been making boomerangs. If the artifact discovered in the mountains of southern Poland in 1985 by Pawel Valde-Nowak and his colleagues from the Polish Academy of Sciences is a boomerang—and they are convinced that it is—then humans have been making boomerangs for a very long time. Valde-Nowak and his colleagues found the crescent-shaped piece of mammoth's tusk along the Białka River in the Tatra Mountains, which lie between Poland and Slovakia. On the same mountain slopes where winter athletes now sweep down on their high-tech skis, the ancients once fashioned this boomerang. This marvel is an example of one type of boomerang: the nonreturning boomerang.

Nonreturning boomerangs—also known as throwing sticks or kylies, as some of the Australian Aborigines called them—have been found all over the world. They were used for hunting and could travel long distances, easily exceeding 150 yards. The tomb of King Tutankhamen (who died more than 3,000 years ago) held another example of this form of boomerang. It is slender and resembles a curved rib. Egyptian throwing sticks were between 10 and 25 inches long and weighed between 2 and 9 ounces. They were used to kill small prey, such as birds. Ancient Egyptians thought the boomerangs could be used in the afterlife to thwart evil spirits who were thought to appear as birds and harm the dead. But the king was well protected: Tutankhamen was an avid duck hunter, and he too used throwing sticks. He was buried with many well-preserved samples of them. The image below depicts ancient Egyptians duck hunting in the marshes in the 15th century B.C. The photo was taken inside the tomb of Nakht, an Egyptian official, who was buried at the Theban Necropolis on the west bank of the Nile River. The ancient Egyptians also used a hieroglyph in their writing system that resembled a throwing stick.

Native Americans of the southwestern United States and northern Mexico, including the Hopi, Zuni, Navajo, and Paipai Indians, had similar throwing sticks, called rabbit sticks, for hunting small prey. These devices have also been found in India, Europe, North Africa, Canada, Indonesia, and Australia. They also have been found in Iraq along the upper Tigris River, where they were used by the ancient Assyrians and Babylonians.

Excellent examples of wooden nonreturning boomerangs have been nicely preserved in peat bogs across Europe (and possibly a few in Australia), along with some unlucky men

An ancient Egyptian hunting ducks with a throwing stick.

and women who fell in with them. Some of these European bog boomerangs date back to approximately 3000 B.C. The oldest physical evidence of boomerangs in Australia was found at Wyrie Swamp in 1973 by Hans van Schaik, the owner of the bog. He had the good fortune of being hospitalized with a kidney stone in the same room with Roger Luebbers, an archeologist. When van Schaik told Luebbers what he had found, Luebbers started digging. The boomerangs found at Wyrie date back to 8000 B.C. The boomerang shown below is 26.7 inches long and weighs 0.8 pounds. This type of throwing stick was used for hunting and fighting.

A throwing stick hieroglyph.

As for returning boomerangs, other ancient peoples may have had such devices, but the strongest evidence for their place of origin is in Australia. The indigenous people of Australia have inhabited the continent for approximately 60,000 years, so they had ample time to experiment with both returning and nonreturning boomerangs. Physical evidence of boomerangs in Australia dates back as far as 10,000 years, and since wood does not last forever, the earliest boomerangs may date back further still.

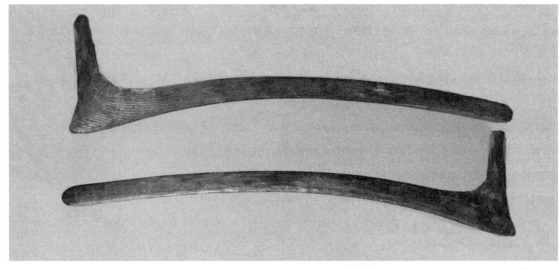

Australian nonreturning hook boomerang.

Recent History

In Australia, the first written account of the flight of a returning boomerang was made by Francis Louis Barrallier, a French-born surveyor and engineer who explored Australia for the British at the start of the 19th century. On its Web site (www.boomerang.org.au), the Boomerang Association of Australia quotes Barrallier's journal entry from November 12, 1802: "They throw it on the ground or in the air, making it revolve on itself, and with such a velocity that one cannot see it returning towards the ground; only the whizzing of it is heard."

The origin of the term *boomerang* can be traced to the Turuwal people, who inhabited the area near modern-day Port Jackson, the harbor of Sydney, Australia. Apparently these people only referred to the returning throwing stick with the word *boomerang*; they used other words to refer to nonreturning throwing sticks. According to the Boomerang Association of Australia, the first written account of the word—"bou-mar-rang"—was made in 1822.

In the United States in the 1950s, the general public did not think about boomerangs very often; people regarded them mostly as curiosities. But an article in the November 1968 issue of *Scientific American* magazine—"The Aerodynamics of Boomerangs" by Felix Hess— helped advance their popularity. Hess covered the physics well, and the accompanying photos, which depicted boomerangs in flight, enabled designers to begin thinking about more advanced designs.

In the early 1970s, boomerang expert Benjamin Ruhe gave several lectures and conducted workshops with the Smithsonian Institution in Washington, D.C. Before they left the workshop, attendees were given unfinished boomerangs. Back home, they would carve them using the skills they had learned. Herb Smith, one of the first high-tech designers of boomerangs, attended the 1976 workshop. He is renowned for his advanced designs and long throws, and he inspired a generation of boomerang enthusiasts to perfect their own designs.

Modern Boomerangs

Modern boomerangs, both returning and nonreturning, come in many different shapes. The boomerangs on pages 7–9 are all Australian boomerangs, except for those in the last photo, which are by English boomerang designer Herb Smith.

On the right side of Herb Smith's long-distance boomerang, there are two small circular marks near the tip. Those are weights that were inserted to increase the boomerang's

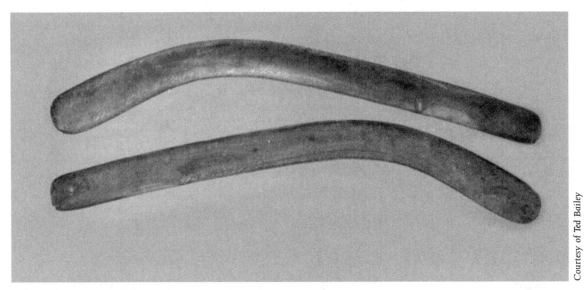

Northern Territory, 1950s, nonreturning (30 inches, 1.2 pounds).

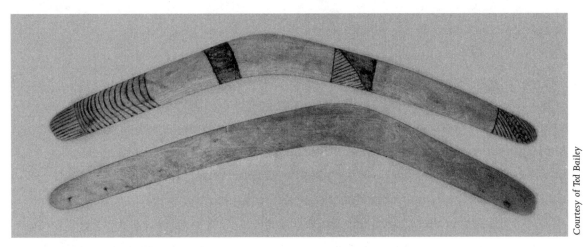

Northern Territory, 1960s, nonreturning.

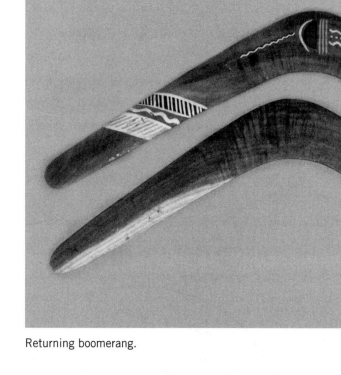

Courtesy of Ted Bailey

Returning boomerang.

range. The effect of these weights will be discussed in chapter 9, "Boomerang Theory." Also, as you can probably tell, Smith's long-distance boomerang is not made of wood. Modern boomerangs are made of some of the following materials: plywood (Finnish birch, Baltic birch, or marine), thermoplastics (polycarbonate, ABS, or polypropylene), composite materials (carbon fiber, phenolic, fiberglass, paxolin, or Kevlar), and aluminum.

A surprising number of different shapes can be made that fly reasonably well. The professional boomerangs on page 10 show some of the exotic and elegant shapes that modern

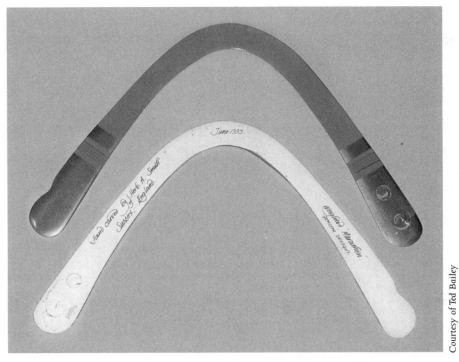

Long-distance boomerangs by the English boomerang designer Herb Smith.

Courtesy of Ted Bailey

returning boomerangs can take, but they are only a few of the most common designs. Some boomerangs are shaped like birds, other animals, question marks, or even letters of the alphabet. These MTA ("maximum time aloft") boomerangs are specially engineered to stay in the air for a long time.

These photographs show how far boomerang technology has advanced in the past 20 years. New materials and more aerodynamic forms are being tested to develop boomerangs that will perform even better in the future.

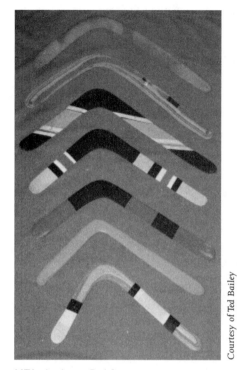

MTAs by Larry Ruhf.

Courtesy of Ted Bailey

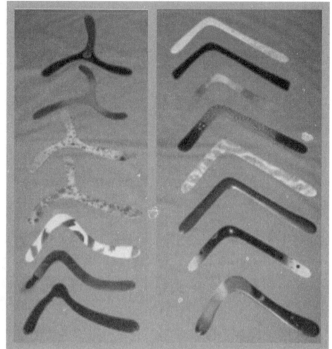

More MTAs.

Courtesy of Ted Bailey

Modern Competition and Records

Professional boomerang championships are a recent occurrence: the first one was held in 1981. Today quite a few more tournaments are held both nationally and internationally.

On March 22, 1997, Sadir Kattan set the world record for flying an incredibly small returning boomerang while competing in the Australian National Boomerang Championship. The boomerang had to go out 20 meters (about 65 feet) and return to a designated spot, called the accuracy circle. His tiny boomerang measured 48 millimeters (1.8 inches) long and 45 millimeters (1.77 inches) wide.

The world's largest returning boomerang was built by Gerhard Walter of Austria and thrown on July 1, 2008. This boomerang, called the Flying Bigfoot Highlander, was 259 centimeters (8.49 feet) from tip to tip, and it weighed 1,092 grams (37 ounces, or 2.3 pounds). At the vertex, where the blades meet, there is a protruding handle. To throw it,

Sadir Kattan

Sadir Kattan with his Guinness World Record flyer.

The world's largest returning boomerang (8.49 feet from tip to tip).

Helmut Lunghammer

Walter holds this handle and cocks the boomerang back until the blade rests against his back, and then he launches it forward. There is a video on the Internet of him flying this and many of his other boomerangs—you can visit my Web site, www.paperboomerangs.com, for a link.

The record for the longest nonreturning boomerang throw was set by David Schummy on March 15, 2005. He threw a lightweight, question mark–shaped boomerang that measured 1,401.5 feet at the Murrarie Recreation Ground in Australia. That's more than a quarter of a mile! There is also a video on the Internet (see www.paperboomerangs.com again for a link) that shows him launching his boomerang and then chasing after it. The problem with a nonreturning boomerang competition is that once the boomerang is thrown, you may never see it again unless you are fast on your feet.

The longest recorded time that a boomerang has stayed in the air was an unofficial record set in 1993 by John Gorsky. His MTA flyer stayed aloft for 17 minutes and 6 seconds. The *official* record for maximum time aloft was set on February 23, 2008, by Betsylew Miale-Gix, an attorney in Seattle. Her flyer stayed up for 3 minutes and 49.82 seconds.

There are many different types of competitive events in the world of boomerangs: MTA, fast catch (the greatest number of catches in five minutes), trick catch (which could involve, for example, catching the boomerang behind the back, under the leg, or with the foot), and doubling (throwing two boomerangs simultaneously and making the catches in prescribed pairs).

The Internet has many videos of interesting tricks performed with boomerangs. One of the most intriguing is from the German-language television show *Wetten, dass . . ?* ("Wanna Bet?"), one of the top-rated shows in Europe. Ordinary people make a claim that they can perform some difficult or strange task and then demonstrate what they can do. For example, a farmer claimed that he could recognize his cows by the sound they made when chewing apples. Bets are placed by the guests attending the performance—past guests have included Mikhail Gorbachev, Hugh Grant, Arnold Schwarzenegger, and Bill Gates. On one show, a man came out on the stage wearing a baseball cap with an apple attached to the top. He hurled a three-bladed boomerang over the audience; it zoomed quickly around the room and returned to chop the apple in half. Some have speculated that the apple was sliced before the man came out on stage and was held together by toothpicks. The video, while a bit silly, is still quite amazing, quirky, and delightful.

Today, boomerang associations keep records on the various formal events that take place all over the world. The following is a short list of these organizations:

- Belgian Boomerang Association
- Boomerang Association of Australia (BAA)
- Boomerang Throwing Association of New South Wales (BTANSW)
- British Boomerang Society
- Danish Boomerang Club
- United States Boomerang Association
- Washington Boomerang Club

There are also many Web sites that sell colorful and well-designed boomerangs.

Out of This World

Would you believe that boomerangs have been flown in space? Astronauts have attempted this act on three separate occasions. Of course, since the boomerangs need air to fly, they were thrown inside each astronaut's spacecraft. The first flight attempt was made in January 1992 by the German astronaut Ulf Merbold on Spacelab. The French astronaut Jacques Thomas threw the second one on the Russian Mir Space Station in 1997. But the third flight was the most successful—it was made with a three-bladed boomerang aboard the International Space Station, thrown by the Japanese astronaut Takao Doi on March 18, 2008. The boomerang was specifically designed to fly under zero-gravity conditions. A video of Takao Doi flying this boomerang is available on the Internet; see www.paperboomerangs.com for a link. There were many people who thought that boomerangs would not fly in zero gravity—they were wrong!

The Silent Sport

It is amazing that there has not been greater interest in this fun sport. Some have called it the "silent sport," but boomerangs are such fun that their popularity will continue to grow. The advances in materials and design have made these gadgets easily accessible to anyone wishing to learn how to throw them. As you will soon learn, one of the simplest ways to make boomerangs is to use paper. Paper boomerangs can be crafted quickly and can be specifically designed to fly in rooms of almost any size, from auditoriums to living rooms.

2
Materials

To build a paper boomerang you need the following materials:

- Railroad board
- Scissors
- Yardstick or ruler
- Stapler
- Glue stick
- Pencil

For convenience, you may also want to use the following:

- Small paper cutter
- Large paper cutter (not shown)

Basic materials.

The additional materials pictured below are not necessary to construct paper boomerangs that fly well, but they will allow you to experiment with a greater range of materials and improve the look of the boomerangs. These materials are only a small sample of the many different types of materials that can be used to make and adorn paper boomerangs.

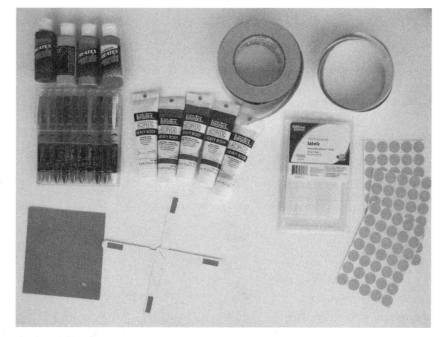

Additional materials.

In addition to the materials described in this chapter, chapters 11 and 12 have a more detailed list of materials, and a more specific explanation of how they are used. Appendix A (page 133) contains lists of materials and where to purchase them.

Paper

Rigid *railroad board* is an inexpensive and excellent paper for making boomerangs. When your boomerangs are made from this paper, they will have a sharp, fast flight. You can buy railroad board at many teacher supply stores and art supply stores. Many elementary schools already have this paper in their supply rooms. Get the 6-ply (6-layer) railroad board. It comes in large 22-inch-by-28-inch sheets and is available in many different colors. CAUTION: See the note about "poster board" on page 135.

Strathmore 500 Series 4-ply bristol board comes in 23-inch-by-29-inch sheets. It is an expensive art paper and is carried by major art supply stores. International Paper also makes a variety of papers that are excellent for making paper boomerangs. The online store at www.paperboomerangs.com carries all of the above papers.

Railroad board.

All these types of paper have a *grain*. For each of these types of paper, you must determine in which direction the grain runs on the sheet. For railroad board—depending on the manufacturer and which parent roll the sheet is cut from—the grain can run along either the 28-inch length of the paper or the 22-inch width of the paper.

Determining Grain Direction

You can find out which way the grain runs by using one of two methods:

Method 1: This is the preferred method. It takes a little practice, but it is very easy to learn. Pick up the sheet so that your left hand grasps the left side of the sheet along the longest side—the short side of the paper should be at the top. Your right hand will be on the opposite long side. Flex the sheet back and forth across the width. Feel the resistance of the sheet to this bending. Then repeat this action across the length of the sheet, this time holding onto the short sides. Flex across the width a few times, then flex across the length a few times. Compare the stiffness in both orientations. If the grain runs along the length of the paper (the longer dimension), it will be more difficult to flex across its length. Conversely, if you meet greater resistance when you bend the paper across its width (the shorter dimension), then the grain runs along the width.

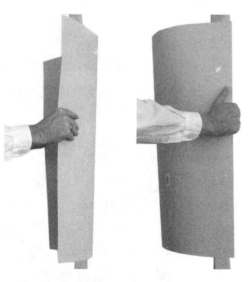

Method 1: Flexing across the width of the entire sheet.

Method 2, Part 1: Cut a ¾-inch-by-8-inch test strip, as shown in the photo below, so that the longer cut runs along the 28-inch length of the sheet.

This 8-inch piece should be rigid.

Method 2, Part 2: Pinch the end of the 8-inch strip between your fingers and wiggle it up and down as shown. If it wiggles up and down loosely, the grain must run along the width of the strip. That means the grain also runs along the 22-inch width of the full sheet. Conversely, if the strip is rigid, the grain runs along the 28-inch length of the full sheet.

The top strip in the photo is rigid, while the bottom is floppy.

Cutting the Paper

Because the grain must run along the length of the boomerang wing (so the wing will be rigid), the 22-inch-by-28-inch sheet will be cut into 8-inch strips so that the grain will run along the width of each 8-inch strip.

If the grain runs along the 28-inch length of the paper, cut the sheet as shown here. You will have three 8-inch strips. A 4-inch strip will be left over—save this strip.

If the grain runs along the 22-inch width of the paper, cut the sheet as shown on the next page. You will have two 8-inch strips. A 6-inch strip will be left over—save this strip.

Other Types of Paper

Before moving on to other types of paper, you should use only railroad board for the first projects. Later designs will stress the use of other types of paper, but when you begin, it's better to limit the variables in the boomerang's design. This will make it easier for you to obtain very consistent flights when you're first learning how to throw.

There are, however, some very interesting papers to consider. For example, as mentioned above, International Paper has many types of cover stock that are excellent for making boomerangs. Different types of paper and their properties will be discussed in chapter 6.

Other Materials

- **Scissors:** Be sure to purchase a good pair of scissors. Choose a pair with about a 4-inch cutting length. They will ensure straight cuts along the length of the blades. Using them helps to prevent accidentally bending the paper while you are attempting to cut it. Consider purchasing a pair by Fiskars that has an ergonomic design. They spread the pressure over the area at the base of the thumb so that you can comfortably cut thick pieces of cover stock.
- **Glue stick:** A small glue stick is all you need. If you use liquid glue to attach the weights to the wing tips, the tips may curve. A glue stick will prevent this from occurring. If the wing tips are curved, the boomerang may veer upward instead of having a flat trajectory.
- **Stapler:** A good stapler is a fast way to attach the blades to each other. Swingline has several types of staplers. For best results, get the slightly more expensive stapler shown on page 17. The stapler should be able to go through at least 20 sheets of 20-pound paper. This will enable you to staple two boomerang wings together with a total thickness of 0.042 inches if you are using the soft 6-ply, 0.021-inch-thick railroad board. Because the Strathmore 500 is a soft paper, the lighter weight Swingline will also staple two pieces of it together (0.048 inches). The stapler should not malfunction when going through two pieces of railroad board, which would be 0.042 inches thick for both pieces. For the advanced hobbyist, the Swingline 390 heavy-duty stapler may be used on paper wings

that approach 0.082 inches in thickness. This stapler uses ⅜-inch staples. For two boomerang wings not exceeding 0.042 inches in thickness, the lighter weight Swingline works fine. If you do not use the stapler, on the lighter weights of paper (0.021 inches, for example) you may use the glue stick, but you will have to wait for the glue to dry completely.

- **Paper cutter:** After cutting the railroad board into 8-inch-wide strips with a pair of scissors or a large paper cutter, a small paper cutter is handy for cutting them into 8-inch-by-¾-inch strips for the wings. You do not need a large paper cutter. You can always use scissors, a yardstick or ruler, and a pencil on the large sheets of railroad board. But when cutting the 8-inch-by-¾-inch wings from the 8-inch-wide swaths, using a small paper cutter rather than the scissors will *ensure that each strip is not bent or twisted while you handle it.*
- **Pencil:** If you have a large paper cutter, you may not need one.
- **Yardstick or ruler:** If you do not have access to a large paper cutter, you will need this to measure the 8-inch-strips before cutting the large sheets of railroad board.
- **Origami paper:** This beautiful and colorful paper can be attached to the paper wings.
- **Photoluminescent tape:** This tape is used for flying paper boomerangs in the dark.
- **Toy gyroscope:** Although this is not needed for the construction of paper boomerangs, it may help you to perfect a deeper grasp of the fundamental notion of angular momentum, a phenomenon that occurs during a boomerang's flight.

3

Quick Construction

If you have built a paper boomerang before but need a quick review, these six steps are all it takes. If this is your first time building one and you are not certain you are up to the task, flip through this brief chapter to build your confidence. For more detailed instructions, skip ahead to chapter 4.

Step 1: Start with two paper wings. Each wing is 8 inches × ¾ inch. The wings are crossed.

Step 2: Place one staple through the area where the wings cross each other.

Step 3: Cut the wings as shown.

Step 4: Cut off the excess paper.

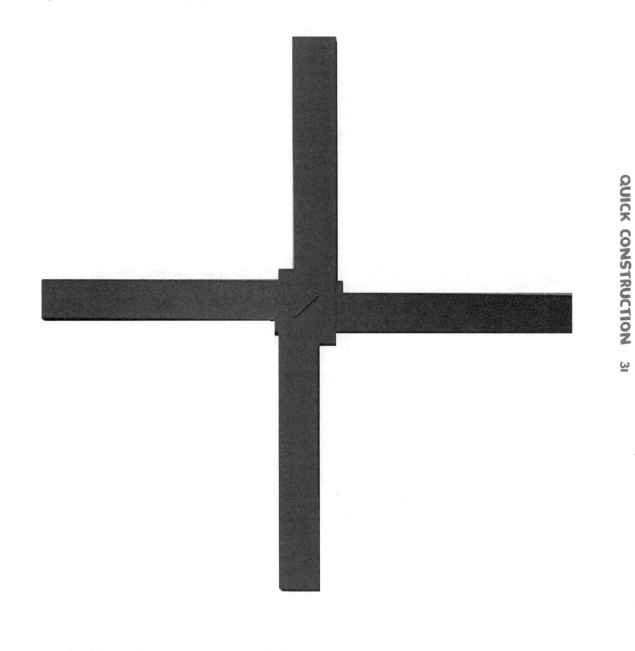

Step 5: Cut the wing tips to make them rounded, as shown. Your trainer boomerang is complete.

Trainer boomerang.

Step 6: Glue small paper weights to the end of each blade. This makes your trainer boomerang a super boomerang!

Super boomerang.

With small variations, this is the process for making a paper boomerang. See, I told you it was easy!

Make a Paper Boomerang

As you will see, this is a very short chapter, but it provides most of the basic information for making paper boomerangs. Anyone can make them by following a specific yet easy-to-understand sequence of steps. Following and practicing these steps will ensure that you are successful every time. However, before discussing these steps, it is necessary to introduce the parts of a boomerang and the motions a boomerang makes as it travels through the air.

Parts of the Boomerang

1. Every paper boomerang has two wings. Each 8-inch-by-¾-inch strip will make a wing.
2. When the two strips (or wings) are crossed, they will make four blades. Call them blade W, blade X, blade Y, and blade Z.

3. Each of the four blades has two edges, a leading edge (LE), and a trailing edge (TE).

4. When the wings are stapled together, the boomerang has two sides: side A and side B. The side where the staple goes in is side A; the side where the staple comes out and curls back against the paper is side B.

Boomerang Fact 1

The boomerang has two kinds of motion: it *spins* on its *axis*, an imaginary line that runs through the center of the boomerang, and *it turns in a wide circle* as it comes back. Engineers call this second motion *precession*.

Boomerang Fact 2

If thrown with the right hand, the boomerang will spin counterclockwise. It should circle the room in a counterclockwise direction until it returns. If you throw it with your left hand, it will spin clockwise, and it should circle clockwise around the room as it returns.

Boomerang Fact 3

With side A facing up, the actual leading edge (LE) of the boomerang will depend on whether the boomerang is thrown with the right or left hand. This is important because the type of cut along the leading edge (the edge that cuts the air) often determines how the boomerang will fly. See the two photos below. Of course, if you flip the boomerang over and throw it with the same hand, the trailing edges (TEs) become the leading edges (LEs).

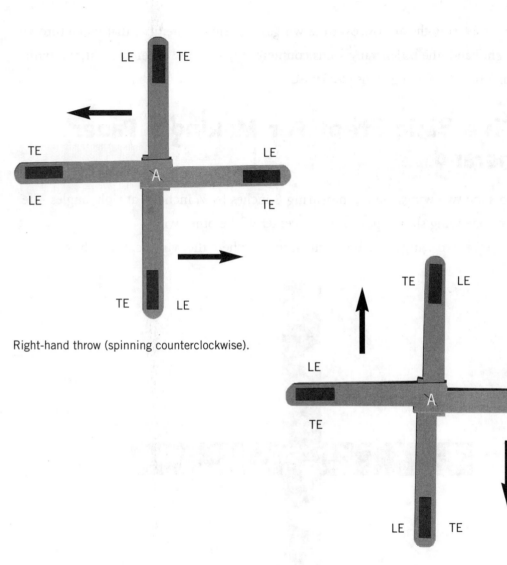

Right-hand throw (spinning counterclockwise).

Left-hand throw (spinning clockwise).

When considering the airflow over the wings, you must remember that when thrown with the right hand, the boomerang spins counterclockwise, and when it is thrown with the left hand, the boomerang spins clockwise.

The Five Basic Steps for Making a Paper Boomerang

Step 1: Cross the two wings—each measuring 8 inches by ¾ inches—at right angles. The center of one wing should pass over the center of the other wing.

Step 2: Staple the two wings together at the middle, where the wings cross each other.

Step 3, Part 1: The following method will help you learn to cut the boomerangs the same way each time. Put the boomerang on a desk in front of you with side A facing up. The first few times you make a paper boomerang, mark the four blades on side A counterclockwise: "W" at the bottom, "X" at the right, "Y" at the top, and "Z" at the left, as shown. If you are using a glue stick to secure the wings, pick a side and mark an "A" in the center of the boomerang where the wings cross. Suppose that you want to make a right-handed boomerang that, when thrown with the right hand, will spin counterclockwise. The photo below shows this counterclockwise movement and also shows which edges of the blades are going to be cutting the air when thrown with the right hand with side A facing up.

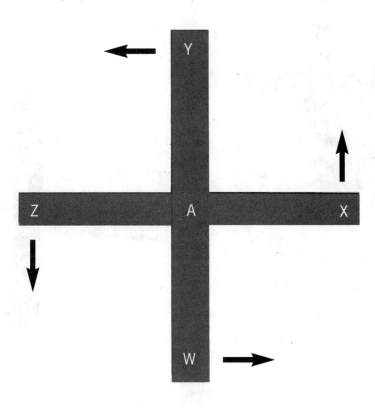

Step 3, Part 2: If you are right-handed, hold the boomerang (side A facing up) in the middle of the blade between your left thumb and left index finger (see the photo below). With a pair of scissors, cut approximately a ⅛-inch strip—but *not more than* ¼ *inch*—off the right side of blade W. Rotate the boomerang *clockwise* and cut the right side of blade X, and so on with blades Y and Z. Cut the blades lengthwise all the way up to the other wing. *Be careful not to curl the wings as you cut them.*

Step 3, Part 3: If you are left-handed, reverse the process and cut the left edge off all the blades.

Step 4: Cut off the excess amount of paper as shown.

Step 5: Round the tips of the wings as shown. This is a trainer boomerang.

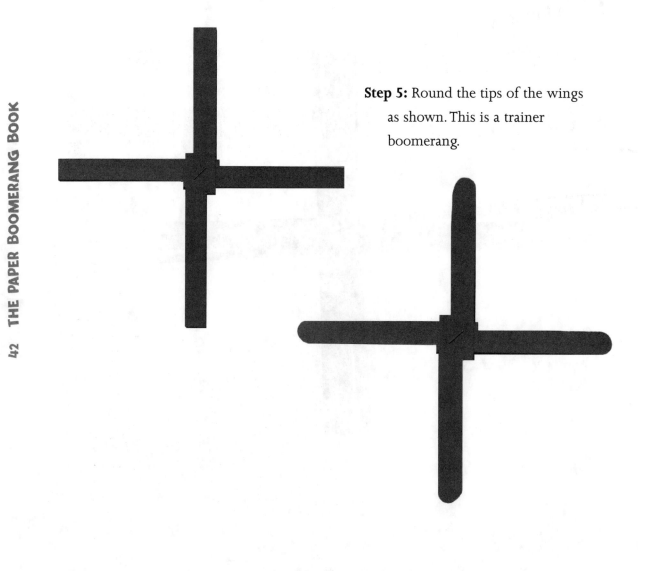

5
Throwing the Trainer Boomerang

The boomerang you just made is a trainer boomerang. It is easier to learn to throw this boomerang than it is to learn to throw the long-distance boomerang, or super boomerang.

The Three Throwing Rules

Wrist-Flick Rule

Hold your hand up in front of you with your palm away from your face as shown in the photo on the left. Without moving your forearm, flick your wrist forward as shown in the photo on the right.

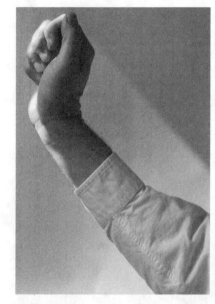
Initial position of the wrist.

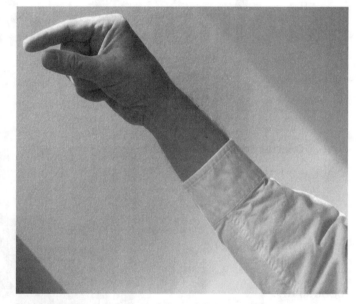
Position at the conclusion of the wrist movement.

Practice moving your forearm and flicking your wrist forward. When you stop the forward movement of your forearm, you should flick your wrist forward. This process puts the necessary spin to the boomerang. See the following pages for photos of the wrist flick.

The photos below, with the hand now holding the trainer boomerang, show the following: (a) that the thumb is pressed against the side of the right index finger at the middle knuckle, and (b) that the initial position of the hand is about a foot away from the right ear. The boomerang should project slightly beyond the back of your head. The girl holding the trainer boomerang at the beginning of this chapter is holding it in the correct initial position.

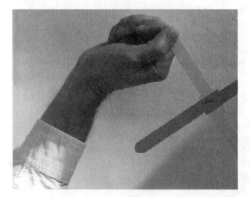

Initial position of the wrist, hand, arm, and thumb.

Final position of the wrist, hand, arm, and thumb.

The Cocking Rule

To properly throw your boomerang, both your boomerang and your wrist must be cocked. When you cock the boomerang, the axis (the center point) moves closer to the spot where your wrist pivots. This action helps put a spin on your boomerang so that it will return to you.

Uncocked boomerang.

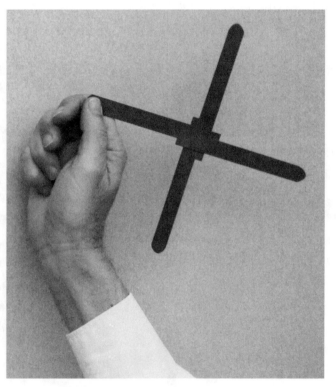

Cocked boomerang.

You will also have to cock your wrist backwards, almost touching the back of your wrist with one of the boomerang's blades, as shown. Hold one tip of the boomerang between your index finger and your thumb.

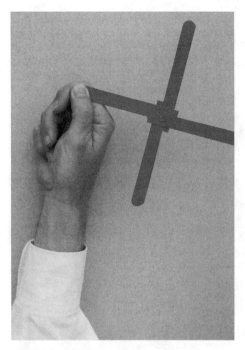

Uncocked wrist.

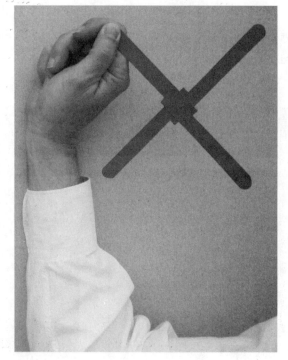

Cocked wrist.

The Tilt Rule

The boomerang will not fly properly if thrown from either of these two positions: (1) at *zero tilt*, when the blades of the boomerang are straight up and down, or vertical; or (2) at *maximum tilt*, when the boomerang is horizontal, or parallel to the ground. Throwing it from position 2 will produce a side throw. If you do a side throw, the boomerang will move upward, turn over, and fly away from you. *Attempting a side throw is the most common mistake people make when throwing.*

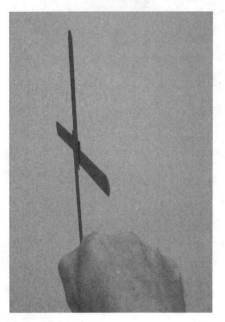

Zero tilt.

Maximum tilt (side throw).

The boomerang must be tilted, from the vertical, away from your body by about 15 or 20 degrees.

Throwing Steps and Practice

Since trainer boomerangs are not weighted, their flight paths will have a smaller circumference than the paths made by weighted boomerangs. Usually you will need an 11-foot-by-11-foot area, but this depends on the type of railroad board you use. Especially stiff railroad board needs a little more space, while railroad board that is not as stiff can be used in a smaller space. If the room is 10 by 12 feet, you may want to throw the boomerang down the length of the room (one of the longer sides), because some flight paths are more elliptical than circular.

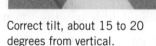

Correct tilt, about 15 to 20 degrees from vertical.

Step 1: Pick up the trainer boomerang by the end of one of the blades. Turn it so that side A is toward you. Cock the boomerang, cock your wrist, and tilt the boomerang to the 15 to 20 degree angle.

Step 2: Aim at a distant spot in front of you and throw the boomerang straight at it, using the wrist flick as you complete the forward movement of your forearm. Later, you may find that you need to aim at a specific place in the air in front of you so that the boomerang will come all the way back.

Step 3: Watch how the boomerang flies. After a successful flight, try to remember exactly how you positioned and moved your body.

Step 4: Repeat steps 1, 2, and 3, but now throw the boomerang a little to the left or right. Watch to see how this change affects the boomerang's flight path.

Step 5: If the boomerang came closer to you by aiming farther left or right, try to remember precisely how you threw it and see if you can do it that way again.

Step 6: Repeat steps 1, 2, and 3, but now aim the boomerang a little higher or lower. Watch what these changes do so you can perfect your throwing style.

Bowing

Sometimes your boomerang's wings can be bowed. This may or may not be good.

Often, when the staple goes through side A, it will cause the paper to curve toward that side. A little bowing toward side A is usually desirable, because it helps ensure that the boomerang will go in the counterclockwise direction when thrown with the right hand. (It's the same on the other side: if the boomerang is thrown with the left hand, the same bow will help it go in the desired clockwise direction.) Sometimes there is no visible bowing—the boomerang seems perfectly flat—and yet the boomerang flies very well anyway.

Correct bowing toward side A.

Watch for these things:

- If the boomerang is bowed toward side B and you throw it with your right hand, instead of going in the expected counterclockwise direction it may veer off in the opposite direction.
- There can be too much bowing, too little bowing, or bowing in the wrong direction. Again, when the bowing is in the wrong direction the boomerang may veer in the opposite direction.
- As the bowing of the wings increases, the diameter of the circular flight path decreases. *The greater the bowing, the smaller the circle*—that is, the boomerang will not go out as far. Of course, you can manipulate the bowing depending on how far out you want the boomerang to fly.
- Too much bowing, especially at the wing tips, may cause the boomerang to veer upward.

Solutions to Three Bowing Problems

If you throw the boomerang with your right hand and it starts off to the right rather than the left, then most likely it is bowed in the *wrong direction.* The bow needs to be curved back toward side A. Follow the finger-sliding technique below to gently bend the blades back toward side A.

Bowing in the wrong direction.

If you have bowed the wings *too much* toward side A, carefully bend them back toward side B to decrease the amount of bowing. If the boomerang flies way out and does not return, bow the wings a little bit more toward side A.

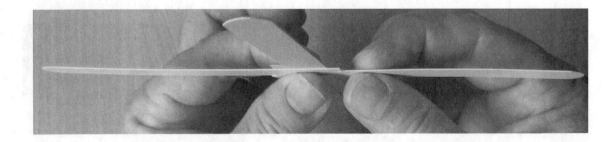

Too much bowing.

Finger-Sliding Technique

This technique will allow you to increase or decrease the curvature of the wings on a trainer or long-distance paper boomerang, which will change the flight path and help the boomerang fly more efficiently. Keep in mind that because the long-distance boomerangs travel farther, their flight paths are more sensitive to changes in the curvature of the wings. You should take great care when using this technique on the wings of a long-range boomerang.

Step 1: With side A facing toward you, pinch the middle of the boomerang (the spot where the wings cross) between your left thumb and left index finger. Your left thumb will be over side A. Now pinch the blade to be bent between your right thumb and right index finger. Your right index finger should be directly over your thumb, as shown in the photo on the previous page.

Step 2: Move your right index finger toward the tip of the blade while leaving your thumb in place. When you look at your fingers from the side, your thumb should be slightly nearer to the center of the boomerang than your index finger. This shift will cause the paper to curl, since your thumb is no longer directly under your index finger.

Step 3: With your thumb and index finger positioned as in step 2, slide your right thumb and index finger toward the tip of the blade and over the section of the blade to be curved or recurved.

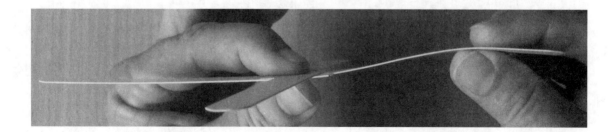

Common Problems and Experimentation

To remember the four most common problems in getting a boomerang to fly right, think "BATS":

B   Bad bowing
A   "A" side not facing you (the curve should be toward side A)
T   Twisted wings
S   Side throw

Most of the issues above have been discussed previously (bad bowing, page 50; side A, page 49; and side throw, page 48). The only one we have not covered yet is twisted wings.

A wing may be warped, lumpy, or twisted. Sometimes you accidentally curl or twist the paper when you are cutting out the wings or when you are cutting the blades length-wise. Most of the time, a twisted wing will have to be discarded. If you're careful, twisting will occur infrequently.

The most common problem when throwing a paper boomerang is failing to correct a side throw. Some people are unaware they are doing it, even after they have seen the proper way to throw the boomerang. Fortunately, it is easy to correct. When you throw the boomerang, check to see that you are not throwing it with a side throw. Also be sure you are not moving your arm or wrist across your chest in front of you. Some people mistakenly flick their wrists sideways. Remember to throw the boomerang straight ahead.

As you develop your throwing style, each time you throw a boomerang you must observe its flight path and keep track of how you moved your body to produce it.

Experimentation: Throw, Observe, Modify

Now that you know how to make and fly a boomerang, you must experiment to improve its flight. Eventually, you will be able to consistently build boomerangs that fly well. But for now, continue practicing until you have mastered the flight of the eight-inch trainer boomerang. Observe it in flight and think about why the boomerang flew the way it did. Form an idea of what you can do to make it fly better. For example, you could modify how you throw the boomerang, how you cut it, or how you shape it after you make it.

Remember, the instructions in this book are for *right-handed boomerangs*. However, these thin paper boomerangs can be thrown with either the right or the left hand. Boomerangs made of wood or other heavier materials are often specifically made for right-handed throwing or left-handed throwing. If you desire to make a left-handed boomerang, make all the cuts along the left side of each blade rather than the right side (see step 3, part 3, on page 41).

The Properties of Paper

It is not necessary to learn the properties of paper to make an excellent paper boomerang. In other words, you may want to skip this section and come back to it later. However, when you experiment, it's helpful to have a more advanced understanding of six paper properties: *rigidity, crispness* or *hardness, mass, volume, density,* and *surface roughness.*

Rigidity or Stiffness

The most important property of paper is rigidity, although you can have a great deal of fun with floppy paper, too. In the paper-manufacturing and paper-converting industry, rigidity is measured in two ways. In the first method, the force it takes to deflect a paper sample of a standard size a given distance is measured. In the second method, a standard force is used to measure the deflection of a standard sample of paper.

A wing with a greater thickness will often have greater rigidity. However, two paper wings made of 0.021-inch railroad board may differ in rigidity, even when they're made by the same company. The dye used to make different colors of railroad board may affect the rigidity of the paper. Black railroad board is usually the stiffest color of 6-ply board. Some colors of paper are denser and harder than others, too (see pages 58 and 59).

Often a less rigid paper wing can be combined with a more rigid paper wing to produce an especially graceful flight. Two rigid wings, however, usually fly a bit faster than two less rigid wings. Paper wings with greater rigidity flex less when the boomerang is

thrown with greater velocity. Paper boomerangs made from more rigid paper are less likely
to veer in unexpected directions.

Crispness or Hardness

When cutting different colors of railroad board with a pair of scissors, one can often tell
how crisp or hard the paper is. If it is crisp or hard, it parts very easily and it has a slightly
greater stiffness. This type of board usually makes the best boomerang fliers.

Mass

Mass is the measure of a body's inertia: the greater the mass of a body, the greater the inertia. What does that mean? It is much harder to push a bowling ball than a golf ball because
the bowling ball has more mass and therefore greater inertia. Inertia is then the resistance
of an object to a change in its state of motion.

Weight, which is a little different than mass, is a force, and it is equal to mass times the
acceleration of gravity. Even though weight and mass are not identical, they are considered
to be so in most practical calculations in physics, engineering, and chemistry. On Earth, all
objects—rocks, trees, people, and boomerangs—have weight expressed in, for example,
pounds, ounces, kilograms, or grams. As you will see, the quality of paper used to make a
boomerang depends on the density of the paper, which is the mass per unit of volume.
Density is discussed further in the sections that follow.

Volume

All stuff takes up space. The more stuff you have, the more space you need to keep it in.
Volume is the amount of space that something takes up. The weight of a standard sample of
paper, along with volume, is used to calculate its density.

Volume is calculated by multiplying length (L) times width (W) times thickness (T):

$$V = L \times W \times T$$

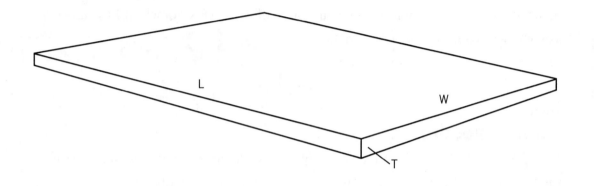

Density

Density is the amount of matter in a given amount of space. A boomerang can be heavier because it is bigger, but it may be heavier not because it is bigger (more volume) but because it is made of something denser.

Imagine two boomerangs that are the same size and shape. They take up the same amount of space, but if you made one boomerang from paper and the other one from a heavy wood, the one made of wood would have more "stuff"—matter—in it for the given amount of space it takes up. It is more dense.

The same is true of two paper boomerangs. Two different types of paper can both be 8 inches long, ¾ of an inch wide, and have exactly the same thickness, but one may be much heavier than the other one. This is because there is more matter in the heavier paper. It has more "stuff" in a given amount of space—to put it another way, the heavier paper has a greater density.

If two paper boomerangs are exactly the same size and you made one out of denser paper, the denser one will usually fly in a larger circle. In this book, density (D) is calculated by dividing the weight of a standard piece of paper (8 x ¾ inches) in grams (g) by its volume in cubic centimeters (cm^3):

$$D = g/cm^3$$

Surface Roughness

Most paper is smooth enough that you will not usually have to worry about roughness. However, one can play with the relative smoothness of paper to obtain interesting differences in the way paper boomerangs fly.

A paper wing that has a smoother surface offers less air resistance, or *drag*. Many manufacturers make cover stock (used for packaging and book covers) of various thicknesses. These papers can be coated or uncoated; they can be coated on two sides (C2S) or one side (C1S). These coatings allow printers to print photographs and text on packaging or book covers. International Paper makes a 20-point (0.020 inches) cover stock called Carolina. Its surfaces are very slick, and it flies very fast.

Different papers have different properties. (See the table below for facts on railroad board.) For a standard sample of railroad board (8 by ¾ inches), the weight, density, deflection (rigidity), and thickness have been calculated. The average weight, density, and deflection of four standard samples were taken for each type of paper. A weight of two grams was suspended from one end of each standard sample, and the deflection was measured. Notice that the black railroad board is the stiffest sample. While the black railroad board is the stiffest, different manufacturers produce boards that vary in stiffness. The stiffest black paper works the best.

The Properties of Railroad Board

Railroad Board Color	Weight in Grams of Standard Piece (8 inches x ¾ inch)	Density (g/cm³)	Deflection (cm)	Thickness (points*)
Black	1.48	0.72	3.0	21
Yellow	1.41	0.68	4.8	21
Red	1.36	0.66	3.8	21
Light Blue	1.59	0.77	3.6	21

* 1 point = 0.001 inches

7

The Little Dragons (Long-Distance Paper Boomerangs)

These paper boomerangs are designed to fly indoors, in rooms of almost any size. All you have to do is put just the right amount of weight on the tips of the wings.

Little Dragon Super Boomerang 1

Step 1: Make a standard trainer boomerang.

Step 2: Using railroad board, cut four 1-inch-by-¼-inch rectangles. The grain should run along the 1-inch length of the rectangle. That is, the rectangle should be stiff to help prevent curling as the glue dries on the wing tips.

Step 3, Part 1: On side A, use a glue stick to glue one rectangle near the tip of each wing, as in the photo below.

Step 3, Part 2: The rectangles are almost at the ends of the wings, but not quite. Also, it is very important to place the paper rectangle in the **middle** of the wing. There is a reason for this: if the rectangle is glued on the leading edge of the wing, it will slow the spinning of the boomerang. If it is placed in the middle, the air flows more smoothly over the wing. Examine the close-up photos on the next page to get an idea of where to place the weights. Make sure each paper weight is flat against the wing by pressing it down after you glue it.

Correct placement (centered).

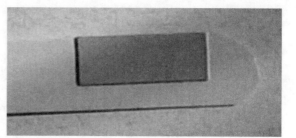

Incorrect placement (not centered).

Step 4: After you have finished step 3, test-fly your boomerang. Be sure to recheck the bowing of your boomerang. A little bowing will usually be all right.

Step 5: This step—trimming the wing tips—may or may not be needed, depending on the results of your test flight. If your boomerang does not come all the way back and you have already checked for bowing of the wings and wing tips, cut a thin slice off the leading edge of each wing. This small trimming usually causes the boomerang to come about a foot or two closer to where you threw it from.

Narrow slice.

Slice removed.

Keep in mind these three things:

1. After the tip of the wing is trimmed, it should not be narrower than ½ inch.
2. The slice should be anywhere from 1 to 2 inches long.
3. Begin cutting halfway between the forward edge of the weight and the leading edge of the boomerang. Do not cut off the entire wing in front of the weight on the leading edge—leave a little wing in front of the weight so that it will smooth the airflow over the surface of the wing.

Little Dragon Super Boomerang 2

Now it's time to make another boomerang, one that has an even greater range. To fly it, you'll need a larger room, such as an auditorium or a classroom. It takes a little more practice to learn to throw the indoor, long-range paper boomerangs, but practicing with trainers and the first type of super boomerang will prepare you.

First, make another trainer. Then go through the same steps you used when making the first long-range boomerang. After you glue the rectangular paper weights on side A, flip the boomerang over and place four more paper weights on side B. Place them in the same way that you did with side A.

Now you're ready to test-fly your boomerang. After your test flights, if the boomerang is not coming back, check for bowing along the wings and at the wing tips and make any necessary corrections. If that does not work, you may have to start over and make a new boomerang.

Remember, different colors of railroad board have slightly different properties. When the paper weights are drying, certain colors of paper may make the wing tips curve slightly more than other colors would. When throwing a long-distance boomerang in a room with a low ceiling, curving at the wing tips will cause the boomerang to rise too high and hit the ceiling. While having a room with a 12-foot ceiling might help, try switching papers.

What you want in a large room with a standard ceiling height is a flat trajectory. You can more often get a flat trajectory by simply switching colors or using two wings of different colors. With some practice designing and throwing these boomerangs, you should be able to build a super boomerang with a flat trajectory nine out of ten times.

8

The Art of Tuning Paper Boomerangs

After you cross the wings and staple them, any adjustment that you make to the paper that changes its shape, degree of smoothness, weight, or weight distribution is called tuning. Ways to tune your boomerang include: (1) cutting along the length of the blade, (2) placing the weights, (3) trimming the wing tips so it will land closer to you, and (4) correcting the bowing. If you have followed the instructions in this book, you have already practiced the art of tuning.

But there are a few more things you may want to consider. Since the wing tips are farther from the center point of the boomerang (the axis about which the boomerang spins), the wing tips are travel-

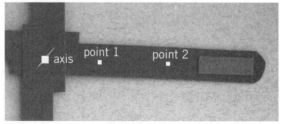

ing faster than points along the wing that are closer to the axis. In the photo above, point 2 will travel faster than point 1.

As the boomerang spins through one revolution, for example, the point farther from the axis point (point 2) will travel around a circle with a greater circumference than the point closer to the axis (point 1). Therefore, any change—even a small, inconspicuous one—around the wing tips will often have a pronounced effect on the flight of your boomerang.

Taped wing tip.

A Guide to Tuning, Experimentation, and the Selection of Materials

Think about the materials you use. Tuning is largely a matter of gaining a better understanding of the materials you are using as you perfect the flights of your boomerangs. Tuning relies on accidental discoveries made during experimentation that are incorporated into the boomerang's design. No matter how rewarding it may be to have a boomerang that flies well, the process of tuning can be considered an art form and an end in itself.

The feel of the paper, the sense of its weight and fragility, are what an experimentalist needs to be aware of to devise appropriate methods and to select the materials for building paper boomerangs. For example, knowing why the wing tips are an especially critical area along the surface of the boomerang might prompt you to tune your design by smoothing the surface of its wing tips. Or, quite naturally, the opposite idea may come to mind—that is, you might want to deliberately roughen the surface of the wing tips. Now you have some experiments to perform. At this point, you may already be predicting and anticipating the results of those experiments.

Labels

Take, for example, increasing the smoothness of the wing tips: Scotch tape can be placed over the weights (as in the photo on page 70) to produce smoother airflow over the tips. This addition increases the weight at the tips, but it also smoothes the surface so that the boomerang spins faster on its axis. Often the tape will cause the boomerang to zip through the air very quickly. Try it—make another Super Boomerang 1, test-fly it, and then place tape over each of the weights. Test-fly it again and observe any changes in the way it flies.

Visit your local office supply stores and look for interesting materials. They have many different materials that you can use. Avery Dennison, a label manufacturer, has many label products that can be used to tune your boomerangs, such as the Avery Easy Peel white address label for laser printers, which comes in different sizes and packages of different quantities.

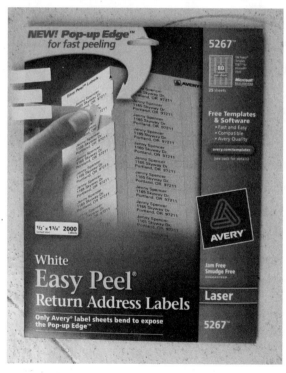

Adhesive labels.

If you use this type of product on white uncoated railroad board, cut a 1½-inch-by-½-inch strip and place it on both sides of the wings near the wing tips. This is a very thin material and even if it is placed across the entire width of the blade from the leading edge (LE) to the trailing edge (TE), the boomerang will fly well. If the label material is placed on both sides of the wing and covers it from the TE to the LE, this boomerang will need to be thrown with a little more force. Still, the boomerang will have a flat trajectory and a beautiful, nearly circular flight path.

Avery also has white return-address labels that are ½ inch by 1¾ inches. These labels are a perfect size and do not need to be cut. With 80 labels per sheet and 25 sheets, you will have 2,000 labels per package. This material is very easy to work with. But in general, if you use any type of label, the returns of your boomerangs will be sharp, flat, and fast.

Adhesive Putty

There are at least two types of adhesive putty: blue and gray. You can perform many experiments in quick succession with this material. Office Depot and other office supply stores have gray, removable putty that you can use for weighting your wings. It leaves a little residue on the paper, but it works very well. (The blue putty leaves less residue.) Small dots of these materials can be used near the tips of your boomerang's wings. They can be easily moved to different locations so that the circumference of the boomerang's flight path can be quickly changed.

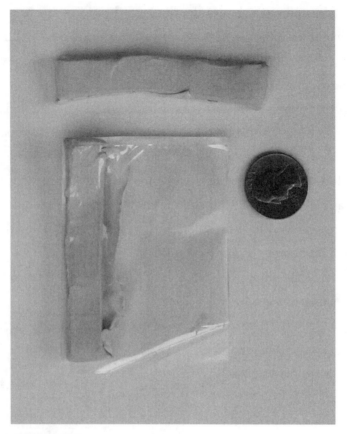

Adhesive putty.

Scissors and Paper Cutters

You have already discovered that the ease with which you can tune a paper boomerang often depends on the properties of the railroad board out of which it is made. As you practice building paper boomerangs, you will also discover that different colors of railroad board have slightly different properties. It is worth repeating that these boards vary slightly in density (weight per unit of volume), hardness, and rigidity. The hardness, or crispness, of the paper often determines how scissors curve the leading edges of the wings when you cut them. The thin edges of the boomerang, especially the leading edges, are extremely important in determining how well your boomerang flies.

When the railroad board is cut along the length of the wing, the scissors form a curve—a small airfoil—along that length. Most of the 6-ply railroad boards available in schools, teacher stores, and art supply stores have a thickness of 0.021 inches. The white board that is sold in stores (along with the colored railroad board) that is coated on one side usually has a thickness of 0.020 inches. Even the slightest difference in thickness between the colored railroad boards of 0.021 inches and white railroad boards of 0.020 inches may cause boomerangs to fly differently.

The photo below shows the edge of a piece of railroad board taken with a digital microscope. This paper was cut with scissors. Notice that, at a magnification of 40x, the top edge is curved down slightly, as shown by the black pen line. This microcurve is about 0.004 inches deep. This small degree of curvature forms an ideal microairfoil and mimics the curvature found on an airplane wing, generating the torque (lift) that is needed. (This will be discussed thoroughly in chapter 9, the theory chapter, page 79.)

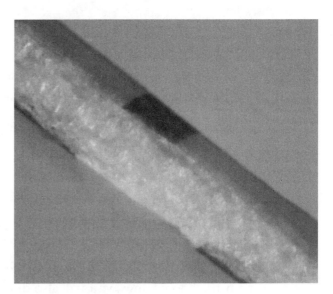

Railroad board edge.

Notice, too, how the bottom blade of the scissors puts a smaller curve on the bottom edge of the paper relative to the top edge. Once again, the leading edges of the wings are very important.

Coated Paper

As mentioned earlier, the surfaces of a boomerang's wings are also important. Uncoated cover stock flies well, but the white coated and uncoated boards fly a little differently. Of course, if the white board is coated on both sides, it may fly quite differently than the uncoated colored railroad boards.

There is one trade-off to consider: a thinner and smoother paper will fly faster, but if it is too thin, the increase in flexibility may cause it to suddenly veer off course and loop in the wrong direction.

Coatings found on paper are often slick. When scissors cut down through this thin layer of material, it causes the leading edge to bend downward just a bit more. This increases the curvature on the edges of the wings. An increase in the curvature of the leading edge can dramatically decrease the air resistance of the wings and cause them to spin quite rapidly. Because of this, the boomerang's energy seems to be more in its spin rather than in its forward movement. This increased spin rate is OK, as long as it does not prevent the boomerang from returning.

As long as you use scissors to make your longitudinal cut to the paper, your leading edges will have the proper amount of curvature. *However, if you cut both the leading edge and the trailing edge with a paper cutter, the boomerang is often more unstable.* It may have a tendency to fly straight ahead (with surprisingly great speed) and hit a wall. When cutting out an 8-inch-by-¾-inch wing, both sides of the wing can be cut with scissors, or it can be cut on one side with scissors and on the other side with a paper cutter.

There is an important point here that bears restating: if you cut the leading edges of the wings with scissors, the angular velocity, or rate of spin, should not be too high to prevent the boomerang from coming back. If the curves on the leading edges of the wings are too exaggerated, the boomerang may make a circle, fall far short of returning to you, flatten out, and float as it is spinning.

To get a better understanding of what's happening, you can make a few 6-inch boomerangs with a file folder. File-folder paper is quite thin and much more flexible than railroad board. Therefore the length of the wings should not exceed 6 inches, or they will flex. Weight the wing tips with two staples placed near the end of each wing. Be careful not to place the metal near the edge of the paper.

Now try to fly one. The wings lack rigidity, so take care not to throw the boomerang too hard. It will probably fly well but crudely when compared to the perfect flights that can be obtained with railroad board. After experimenting with this model for a while, bend the leading edges of each wing down slightly with your fingernail. This bend is almost imperceptible. Fly it again. Most of the time it will not come back, but instead it will spin rapidly and float beautifully in space.

Perfecting the Return

As it returns to you, a paper boomerang made of railroad board will have one of three basic orientations:

1. Slow and flat, with side A facing up

2. Slower, with side B facing you

3. At high velocity with a sharp angle, and with side A facing you

This last photo depicts the ideal, preferred return. If you follow the instructions in the first part of this book, nearly all your boomerangs will have close to ideal orientation as they return to you. This is very easy to do, and it will be rewarding to see how gracefully your boomerangs fly.

9

Boomerang Theory

It is not necessary to understand the physics behind a boomerang to make an excellent paper boomerang, but it does help a little when you are doing experiments and want to push out the edge of your knowledge a little further. For advanced students who want to explore the math and physics of flight, boomerang theory includes the engineering of propellers and the lift created by thin airfoils, which is explained with partial differential equations (calculus). Even the mathematical formulas of the basic physics of boomerang flight involve double integrals.

Of course, part of the fun, beauty, and intellectual richness of studying boomerangs lies in examining the complexities of their flight. You can pursue the theory to a truly advanced level, but fortunately it does not take a lot of theory to grasp how these little flyers work.

This chapter is relatively easy to understand and should provide you with a solid grounding in the fundamentals of physics necessary to understand why boomerangs fly the way they do. If you want to read a more detailed account of the physics involved, go to my Web site, www.paperboomerangs.com. Later in this chapter, I will discuss gyroscopes and the fundamentals of airfoils.

The Basics

A boomerang has two motions: (1) it rotates about an axis, and (2) it travels along a nearly circular, or elliptical, flight path through the air. To understand what's going on below, two blades of the boomerang are labeled tip A and tip B.

A paper boomerang spinning on a desk.

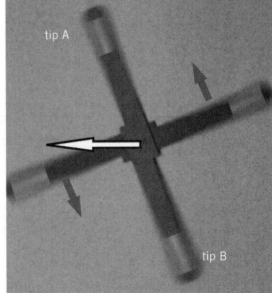

A boomerang's forward movement, plus spinning.

Suppose a boomerang is spinning on its axis while resting on a desk, as shown at left above. In this case, the boomerang has no forward movement and the velocity of tips A and B is determined by the radius of the boomerang (r) and the rate of spin (ω), also known as its *angular velocity*. The faster the boomerang spins, the higher the velocity of its wing tips. In this case, at a constant rate of rotation, the tips A and B are traveling at the same velocity—$r(\omega)$—where ω is the angular velocity, and r is the radius length to the wing tips.

Now imagine that the boomerang is traveling forward in space as it spins counterclockwise. The velocity of tip A now has *two* components, one caused by the spin of the boomerang—$r(\omega)$—and one caused by the forward movement of the boomerang—$v_{(forward)}$. In other words, tip A is moving *faster* than it did just spinning on the desk. Add the velocities together to get the following:

$$v_{(tip\ A)} = v_{(forward)} + r(\omega)$$

Tip B is traveling in the opposite direction as tip A, so it travels *slower* than tip A:

$$v_{(tip\ B)} = v_{(forward)} - r(\omega)$$

Therefore, in the photo on the right on page 80, tip A is traveling faster through the air than tip B.

This difference in tip speeds has major implications. When air travels over the wing of an airplane (or boomerang), the special curvature of the wing, called an *airfoil*, causes *lift*. The faster air flows over the wing, the greater the lift. Since tip A is moving faster than tip B, it has greater lift. This force pushes upward on tip A stronger than on tip B, creating a *torque*, or twisting force, caused by the differences in lift.

Because the boomerang is spinning around a central point, it resists this torque. This force (that resists the torque caused by lift) is caused by the *mass* of the boomerang spinning at a distance from its *axis*. With a given spin rate, the greater the mass near the wing tips, the greater this force—called *moment of inertia*—is. If you spin a toy gyroscope in your hand and try to rotate it in space, you will feel resistance to this motion caused by the gyroscope's moment of inertia.

Toy gyroscopes.

The spinning boomerang is actually a simple gyroscope—most of its mass spins at a distance from its axis, so it resists any change in its direction. When you increase the weights on the blade tips, it creates a greater moment of inertia, which causes the boomerang to fly farther out as it takes longer for the lift force on the wings to overcome this greater moment of inertia.

The constant lift on the wing tips creates a torque that is opposed by the moment of inertia of the spinning boomerang. Together these two forces cause the boomerang to *precess*, or fly in a circular path in space.

Try a little experiment: make a trainer boomerang and place the weight in the *center* of the boomerang rather than near the wing tips. Try a few test flights. What happens?

A Brief History of the Gyroscope

Johann Bohnenberger made the world's first gyroscope in 1817. In the 1850s, after observing the motion of a gyroscope, French physicist Leon Foucault coined the modern word by using the Greek word *gyros*, which means "ring," "circle," or "spiral."

When the great mathematician Pierre-Simon Laplace observed the gyroscope, he thought it could be used to teach classical physics (which is how it is commonly used today). After the Chandler Company first produced the gyroscope as a toy in 1917, generations of children have come to enjoy its curious behavior.

Since boomerangs precess much the same way gyroscopes do, you can develop a deeper knowledge of the motion of a boomerang by observing the odd behavior of a gyroscope. Once again, a fairly detailed presentation of the physics of gyroscopes, and lift, can be found on www.paperboomerangs.com. The concepts of torque, vectors, angular momentum, applied torque, and angular velocity are all discussed. Newton's laws and Daniel Bernoulli's work are also used to explain the motion of boomerangs.

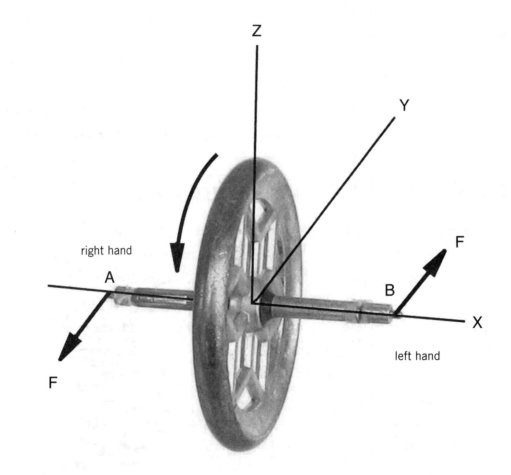

A precessing gyroscope. See it in motion at www.paperboomerangs.com.

Basic Airfoil Design and Vocabulary

It's time to look at a boomerang's wing up close. This section contains the drawings and vocabulary you need to gain a simplified understanding of wing design and its relation to lift and drag.

Find the following terms on the illustration below:

1. **Chord line:** a straight line from the leading edge to the trailing edge
2. **Camber line:** Also known as the *mean camber line*, a plotted line from the leading edge (LE) to the trailing edge (TE) where each point along the line is halfway between the top and bottom surfaces of the wing
3. **Maximum camber:** the maximum distance of the camber line from the chord line
4. **Thickness:** the maximum thickness of the wing

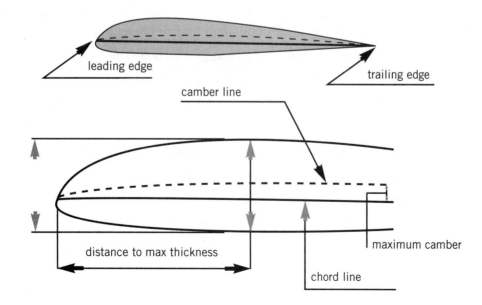

There's one more term that's illustrated below: **angle of attack**.

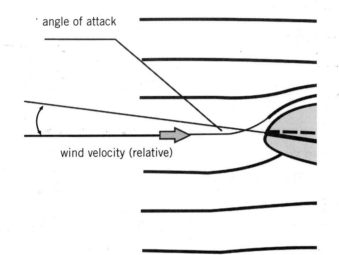

A wing's angle of attack describes the orientation of its chord line relative to the air passing over it. If you increase the angle of attack, you increase the wing's lift. But if the angle of attack is too great, the flow of air over the wing "breaks away" from the surface, and the wing stalls—it doesn't have enough lift. If the wings stalled on an airplane, it would lose altitude very rapidly.

In much the same way as an airplane flies, sometimes it is necessary to turn a boomerang to increase its angle of attack. With a paper boomerang that is properly cut, one that has the appropriate curves on the TEs and LEs, it is not necessary to increase the angle of attack by turning the wings at a slight angle to the forward movement of the boomerang. But sometimes this approach may help with a tricky paper boomerang.

Finally, it is important to understand how air itself flows over a wing. Smooth airflow over the surface of a wing helps to create lift by maintaining a higher velocity of flow—and thus a low pressure—over the wing. But turbulence over the wing can break this flow and decrease the lift.

When discussing airflow, engineers and scientists use the concept of *streamlines*. Streamlines are curves (as in the illustration below) that, from left to right, represent the flow of air toward, over, and under a wing. Streamlines may be thought of as snapshots of the path that moving particles take as they pass over an object, such as a wing. If the path is steady, the airflow is said to be *laminar*, or smooth and layered. Streamlines can bend, but they never cross.

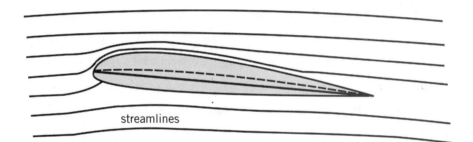

streamlines

The *boundary layer* is the streamline that is closest to the surface of the wing. This layer is extremely important with a paper boomerang. The air velocity at the boundary layer next to the wing's surface is zero. The boundary layer is thin, but it extends out a short way where it is adjacent to another streamline. There is a gradient of velocities of airflow within this boundary layer and at its outer reach; part of it assumes the velocity of the streamline in its local area.

Think of streamlines when you think of the air flowing over the wings of a paper boomerang. There are times when a paper boomerang is very unstable. This instability usually occurs because the leading edges of its paper wings are rough or inappropriately curved. The paper is usually anywhere from 0.020 inches to 0.024 inches thick, so one has a very flat wing except for the small curves at the TEs and LEs. When the boomerang is thrown, it may swiftly veer in an unexpected direction and perform so poorly that you'll think the paper will never fly. But I can't emphasize this enough: *the edges are critical in producing laminar airflow over and around the wings.*

Drag is the final notion to consider about airflow. When a solid object moves through air, its motion is resisted by the air that has to move out of the way. This opposing force is called *drag*. A wing with smooth, laminar flow over it has less drag than one without. Drag on a wing is a complex matter, but there are at least two major components: skin friction and form drag. (There can also be swirling air vortices at the wing tips resulting from the lift. This type of drag is called *induced drag*, though we won't talk about it here.)

A high amount of *skin friction* is caused by a rough wing surface. A wing with a smooth surface will move more easily through the air because it will encounter less resistance to its forward movement. A paper boomerang made with a smooth, coated cover stock will zip through the air a little faster than a boomerang that does not have this coating.

Form drag is created by an object's frontal area—the part of the object that faces into the wind or flow of air. A solid body with a larger frontal area will have a larger amount of drag than a body that has a smaller frontal area. When you place thicker paper weights near the wing tips of a paper boomerang, it increases the frontal area of the wing and therefore increases the drag. This often causes the boomerang to spin at a slower rate. However, for a given weight, a thinner paper with greater density can be used, which will allow the boomerang to spin faster. With thinner and denser wing weights, the boomerang will also usually have a higher forward velocity.

Putting It All Together

So why does a boomerang fly the way it does? There are two reasons. The first is a mysterious gyroscopic force called *reactive torque*. To understand it, let's study the illustration on page 90. The flat disk represents a boomerang flying in space. Look at the area on the disk marked "greatest lift." As the boomerang moves forward, the air on the right side flows over the right blade faster than it does over the blade on the left. Both blades create lift, but there will be greater lift on the right side of the disk, or over the right blade. That twists the disk upward on the right side, out of the page, toward the viewer.

But now something truly extraordinary happens. Even though the right side of the boomerang is twisted upward by lift, it does not actually move upward. Instead, the front of the boomerang, the area near the top of the page, rises! How is this possible? Because the boomerang acts just like a spinning gyroscope.

Look at the illustration on page 91. This is how a spinning boomerang is oriented in flight. Notice that the boomerang is spinning counterclockwise. Look at blade tip H and then look at the opposite tip at the other end of the same blade. Notice the two arrows. The arrow at tip H is bigger because the lift force at that tip is greater than the lift at the other end of the same blade. That blade is being twisted in the direction of the big arrow labeled "net lift." But here, too, tip H does not move in the direction of the arrow. Amazingly, it is **tip B** that moves toward the viewer, because of reactive torque. Only spinning objects behave in this way.

The second force that contributes to turning the boomerang is the lift force. The lift from the wings moves the boomerang to the left and helps to turn it in a circle.

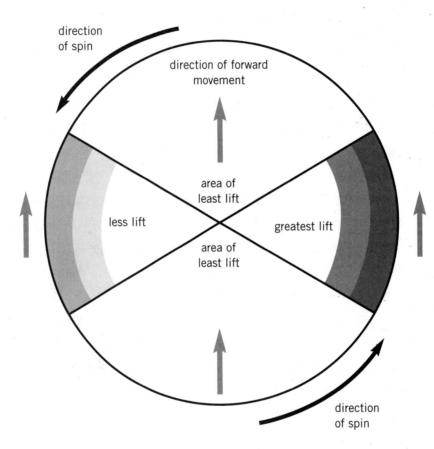

direction of spin

direction of forward movement

area of least lift

less lift

greatest lift

area of least lift

direction of spin

Lift gradient for a rotating blade at different angles to the airflow over the boomerang's wings.

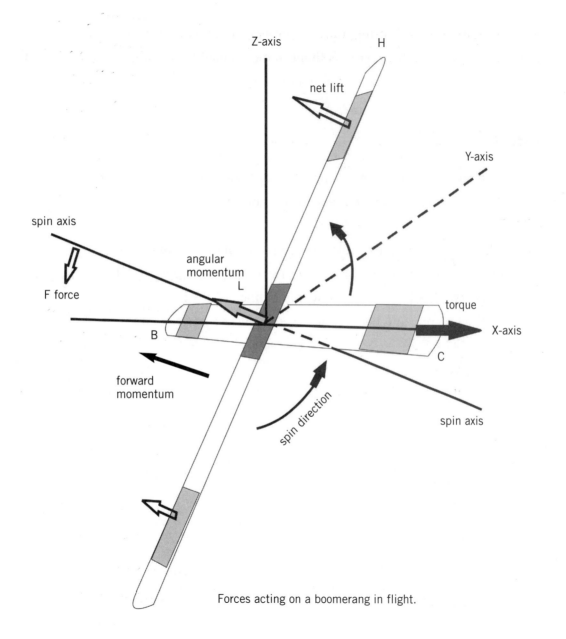

Forces acting on a boomerang in flight.

If you're interested in learning more, www.paperboomerangs.com will take you through the physics of a boomerang's flight in more detail so that illustrations such as the ones in this chapter can be understood in even greater depth.

Learn by Doing

For readers who want to explore the dynamics of boomerang flight using mathematics and physics, a thorough program of experimentation will provide many hours of conceptual fun.

To further explore the gyroscopic effect, a small, high-speed (12,000 rpm) demonstration gyroscope is listed in appendix A (page 139). This gyroscope has a long axle, and it is shown on page 82. It will lean over to within an inch of the tabletop then precess around in a circle, all while resisting being pulled to the table's surface.

10
Tricks and Throws

Mastering the basic throw was easy. Now you are ready to get fancy. The tricks and throws shown in this chapter range from extremely easy to very challenging. Read through the descriptions of the tricks and throws and practice the simplest ones first. But since the list of tricks and throws is far from complete, you may want to experiment and perfect your own tricks. Don't forget to visit my Web site, www.paperboomerangs.com, for videos, descriptions, and still photos of how the professionals throw boomerangs.

Throw 1: The Single-Handed, Forward, Single-Boomerang Throw

The simplest boomerang throw is the single-handed, forward, single-boomerang throw, the first throw you learned in this book. One boomerang is thrown with either the left or right hand. It is thrown with a forward movement of the wrist, forearm, and upper arm.

Some people have a tendency to throw the boomerang like a baseball by moving their upper arms too much, but most of the force needed can come from the wrist and the forearm. However, some paper boomerangs, especially the ones fashioned from double-coated Carolina by International Paper, can often be thrown with great force and return very quickly, even after a little weight has been placed at the tips of the wings to increase the angular momentum. This fast throw is a little tricky, but it is possible to throw them quite hard.

Notice that the model should have cocked the boomerang a little farther back. Also, his wrist should be cocked a little farther back. At this point, though, his arm and wrist are coming forward, so the initial position of his boomerang and his wrist were probably correct.

Throw 2: The Single-Handed, Forward, Double-Boomerang Throw

Of course, anytime you throw two boomerangs simultaneously, it takes some practice to catch them. But, surprisingly, this throw is quite easy and a lot of fun. You can do this throw with the trainer or the long-distance paper boomerangs.

You might experiment with using both a trainer boomerang and a super boomerang together. Imagine two boomerangs, one flying in a larger circle than the other—it might give you a little more time to catch the second boomerang when it returns. The greater difficulty here is in performing the initial throw so that the final positions of the boomerangs make them easy to catch.

One final comment: notice that the boomerangs are not directly on top of each other. Sometimes this arrangement helps to prevent them from hitting each other in flight. But with some boomerangs, placing one on top of the other seems to work a bit better. The difficulty in doing this is that when the boomerangs are overlapped yet still have a little distance between them, the air flows between them and creates low pressure, drawing them to stick to one another in flight. Occasionally this happens, but most of the time they will fly without bumping into one another. This throw is really fun to do, but you will have to be quick.

Throw 3: The Single-Handed, Backward, Single-Boomerang Throw

This throw may be easier to do with a trainer boomerang. It can be difficult to maintain the appropriate tilt when throwing backhanded. However, it is easier to do with a trainer that has slightly wider wings. But you should, with practice, be able to perfect it with a long-range boomerang.

Throw 4: Single-Handed, Backward, Double-Boomerang Throw

This throw is usually easier to do using trainer boomerangs. You may have to make the wings a little wider while keeping the length at 8 inches. Notice the position of the model's wrist. Ideally, his wrist should come backward a bit more so that he can effectively snap his wrist forward. It may be possible to perfect this throw using the long-distance boomerangs, but it will take a good bit of practice. Again, maintaining the appropriate tilt while doing a backhanded throw is the most difficult part of performing this throw.

Throw 5: The Double-Handed, Forward, Single-Boomerang Throw

Throw 5 is easier to do with a trainer boomerang. If you are right-handed, you will need to practice throwing with your left hand. The difficulty here is keeping just the right amount of tilt for the boomerang in your left hand. It may be possible to perfect this particular throw, but it will take a lot of practice.

Throw 6: The Double-Handed, Forward/ Backward, Single-Boomerang Throw

This throw, for some reason, is easier to do than its forward-handed version. It works well with trainer boomerangs that have wings wider than ½ inch. Notice that the model's wrists are not positioned far enough backward (toward him) to allow for a vigorous back-handed snap forward. Also, the boomerangs need to be cocked toward him a bit more.

Using this throw, I have caught both returning boomerangs. But this throw takes additional practice with the hand positions. The boomerangs may not need to be held in the usual way—instead you can hold them with the tips of your fingers. Recall that for forward throws, the boomerang is held between the thumb and the middle knuckle of the index finger. This position ensures that the center of the boomerang, where the wings cross, is closer to where your wrist pivots, which helps impart the necessary degree of spin. With backward throws, where the wrist is curved backward so that the palm is toward what is usually the underside of the forearm, the wrist (with the backhanded snap) is capable of imparting additional spin and velocity to the boomerang.

Throw 7: The Double-Handed, Forward, Double-Boomerang Throw

This throw is a mouthful to say and more than a handful to catch. In fact, you would probably have to be an octopus to pull this one off! But for anyone who wants a challenge, I included it as a possible variation. You will have to catch two with one hand and two with the other. Good luck!

Throw 8: The Double-Handed, Backward, Double-Boomerang Throw

As with the previous throw, you would have to be a true virtuoso to do this. I have no doubt it can be done, but, just as it takes years to play a musical instrument well, it would take the same degree of effort to perfect this trick.

Throw 9: The Over-the-Shoulder Throw

This throw is easy to do either with a trainer or a long-distance boomerang. As the name says, you throw the boomerang over your shoulder. Given that the boomerang is thrown with the right hand, it goes along its path in a counterclockwise direction as you turn to catch it. This is simple to do and, again, great fun.

Throw 10: The Under-the-Leg Catch

If you are fairly limber, you will enjoy this one. This catch is also entertaining and easy to do.

Throw 11: Boomerang Juggling

Boomerang juggling can be lots of fun, but for this one you will need to be quick and you will need an auditorium.

Start by making two very-long-range boomerangs. To juggle them, throw one and pause. As the boomerang returns, throw the second, and catch the first. As the second returns, throw the first, and so on. You will have to aim the boomerangs just right so that you don't have too far to run. Each boomerang must return exactly to you, or you will end up getting a considerable amount of exercise.

For this trick to work well, you should experiment with different types of paper and fashion the boomerangs so as to minimize the distance you have to travel to catch them. Also, try not to get too excited if one of the boomerangs is returning a little faster than you thought that it would—it is easy to throw the second boomerang off course for the whole next cycle.

A Few Final Thoughts

Even though the photos in this chapter were taken outside, the paper boomerangs in this book are **indoor** boomerangs. Air conditioning in a room can alter the flight path of a paper boomerang. But as long as you fly them inside, away from the air vents, they will fly exceptionally well.

11
Artwork and the Paper Boomerang

Now that you've mastered the construction and throwing of the paper boomerang, you probably want to decorate your flyer so that it matches the grace with which it flies. You can draw on the paper or print out designs from your home computer. You can visit my Web site, www.paperboomerangs.com, where you will find numerous examples of interesting designs that you can download. You can print these designs on very thin photo paper or try printing them on thin white origami paper. You then can attach them to larger sheets of railroad board with spray adhesive. Remember, try to keep the wings *thin*.

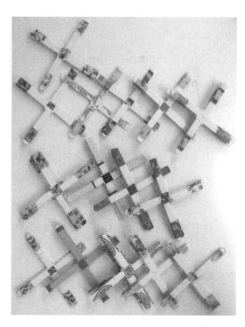

The Glow-in-the Dark Paper Boomerang

Centuries ago the Australian Aborigines discovered the fun of flying boomerangs at night. They would carve out small holes at the tips of their boomerangs, fill them with glowing embers from a fire, and launch them. The rush of air over the embers would cause their boomerangs to glow brightly as the tips emitted a trail of sparks.

Here's a less flammable version you can try: a glow-in-the dark paper boomerang that's an odd hue of green. Identi-Tape (www.identi-tape.com/phosphor.htm) carries various lengths and widths of adhesive photoluminescent tapes. These tapes can be charged with any type of light, but fluorescent lights work very well. The tape charges in about five minutes. This company usually requires that you buy a larger quantity of the tape, but RideSafer (www.ridesafer.com/Glow_Tape_s/45.htm) carries the 1-inch-wide tape, and it can be purchased in small lengths for around $5.

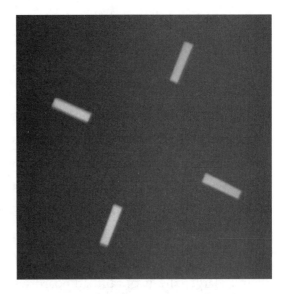

Place a length of the tape near the tip of each blade. Charge the tape under a lamp or in the sun, then turn out the lights. Fly the boomerang in the usual way. The spin and flight path of the boomerang will make it appear as if a green circle is flying around the room. The glow should be bright enough to enable you to catch the boomerang with ease. This is even more fun when several people fly them in a large, dark room at the same time.

Always consider that any adhesive material that is placed on the wing may, in time, curve the boomerang's wing tips. Any material placed on the wing may, depending on its properties, expand or contract. It is possible to select materials that have different rates of expansion (depending on, for example, changes in temperature) than the paper from which the boomerang is made. The adhesive itself may also contract and curve the tips. A little experimentation may be needed, but in general this tape usually works quite well.

Spin, Color, and Design

If you fasten the wings of a paper boomerang together with a stapler, an interesting thing happens: the boomerang can be spun rapidly on any smooth surface, balancing on the raised bumps formed on the side of the paper where the two ends of the staple bend against the paper. If you draw bright colored lines of the same color on the blades, each an equal distance from the center of the boomerang, they will form a circle of color when the boomerang spins. Strong, contrasting colors make interesting patterns of concentric circles. Bright, primary colors and complimentary colors can produce some startling visual effects while spinning. As you paint the lines, spin the boomerang occasionally to test the visual effect so that you can decide which color to use next and where to place it. You can also blend colors so that they gradually change from one area to the next, creating some impressive designs.

The Application of Colors and Designs

If you want your boomerangs as elegantly colored as a butterfly, try origami paper. It comes with many designs and also with bright, solid colors. This paper is extremely thin and usually colored only on one side. Strips of this paper can be affixed to the length of a large sheet of white railroad board. Use spray adhesive on the back of the strip and a rubber roller (called a brayer) to firmly press this decorative paper to the railroad board. Origami paper comes in just about an infinite number of colors, and metal origami foil is also available.

Some types of origami paper are a little thicker. Cutting these thicker papers leaves a slight fuzz along the edge. If you use this paper near the tips of the wings, it will cause your boomerang to rise upward, so it is better to paste this paper near the center of the boomerang. At the back of this book you'll find Web sites where you can purchase origami paper.

You can apply color and designs to a paper boomerang's wings in a variety of ways. One of the simplest methods is to paint on the thick paper stock. You can apply acrylic paints to the surface of the large sheets, then cut them into the appropriate lengths for the wings.

Color can also be printed on labels with an ink-jet printer and applied to the wings, or it can be printed on heavy-weight matte photo paper. Since the color on the labels tends to be a little flat, you might try 44-pound (8½ by 11 inches) Epson matte premium presentation paper. It is heavy enough to increase the boomerang's angular momentum, especially if you place it on both sides of each wing, near the tips. The entire sheet of photo paper can be colored and patterned as desired. Strips can be cut from the photo paper and applied along the edges of large sheets of railroad board. Individual wings can then be cut from this sheet.

There are also many thin, brightly colored papers that can be cut and used as weights at the wing tips, increasing the boomerang's angular momentum. These papers can be purchased in 8½-inch-by-11-inch sheets through paper suppliers such as Xpedx (www.xpedx.com). Xpedx has an excellent selection of 10-point colored papers. But for exceptionally bright colors, origami paper is the product to use.

Straight-Through Ink-Jet Printers

This type of printer is an expensive option, but using it is a quick way to print images and designs directly on your paper. Straight-through printers are used for thick, relatively inflexible types of paper. Most printers can handle only thin sheets of paper that follow a curved path through the printer. With a straight-through printer, the sheets follow a straight path through the printer without bending. I used an Epson R2400 ink-jet printer, but it has since been discontinued. You might want to look at the similarly priced Epson Stylus Photo R2880 ink-jet printer. It has a straight-through path that can be used with thick media that measures up to about .050 inches thick, though you really will not need paper thicker than about .024 inches. The inks for these printers are expensive, but the images are clear and the color quality is very good.

Sometimes the coatings on different papers are not compatible with the inks used in ink-jet printers. The surface of a coated paper may have to be prepared with, for example, a clear digital ground like the one offered by Golden Artists, Inc. This "ground" is a liquid that is poured into a flat plate, rolled with a small rubber roller (called a brayer), and applied to the coated paper. This will help prevent the inks of an ink-jet printer from bleeding into one another.

If you use an ink-jet printer, try visiting Canon's Creative Park Web site (http://cp .c-ij.com/en/). This site has extremely colorful origami designs for paper. If you go to the "Art" menu and select "Chiyogami," you'll find the most subtle colors and beautiful designs. Because they are copyrighted, you should read the terms of use, but you can always use them for a noncommercial purpose, such as making a boomerang for your own use. If you use a coated cover stock, you will have to prepare the surface as described above because the ink will not set correctly on this coated paper. It really takes a long time to dry. Some uncoated paper stocks work quite well. Use an uncoated white cover stock or something similar to the smooth Strathmore 500 Series 4-ply bristol board.

Visual Samples of Paper Boomerangs and Artwork

To view color samples of different types of artwork, please visit www.paperboomerangs.com. The first samples you'll find are designs for printing on large 8½-inch-by-11-inch sheets of paper. Here are two examples:

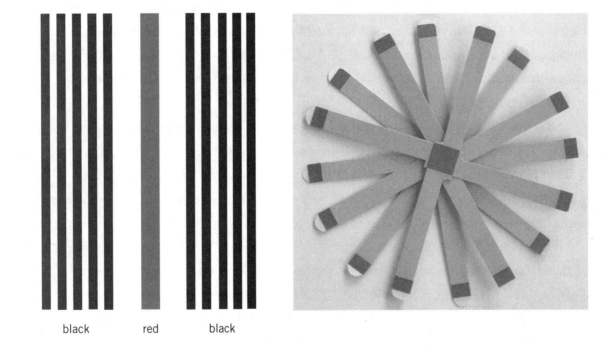

black   red   black

Notice that strong patters that can be created with simple, straight lines. When a boomerang is spinning, anything printed on the blades will form concentric circles. To get a better idea of what these patterns look like, see www.paperboomerangs.com.

12
Paper Boomerangs of Different Sizes

So far this book has only covered the construction of 8-inch paper boomerangs. There are so many different types of paper and so many different ways to construct paper boomerangs that it was necessary to focus on the size used to make the trainer boomerang. But now that you've mastered construction and throwing, it's time to look at other ways to make paper boomerangs of different sizes.

This chapter will explore how to make 6-inch, 7-inch, 9-inch, and 10-inch boomerangs. If you have read everything in this book up to this chapter, you undoubtedly have done a considerable amount of experimentation. You are now prepared to design and build these models, so you will be given a minimal amount of instruction and you can fill in the rest with the fine-tuning skills you've learned.

Shorter Paper Boomerangs: The 6-Inch and 7-Inch Boomerangs

Six-inch paper boomerangs are nifty little flyers. When making shorter boomerangs, you must shrink the wing's width in proportion to the decrease in its length. This will require some experimentation. You must find the optimal width for the given length of 6 inches. For paper thicknesses from 0.020 inches to 0.021 inches, consider the following line of thought: since the optimal width of an 8-inch boomerang is around ½ inch, a 6-inch boomerang would be ⅝ (or ¾) the width, or ⅜ inch wide (since ¾ times ½ equals ⅜). Using this estimated width as a guide, the actual optimal size can be found experimentally. It may be a little less than this, but the measure is probably quite close.

If your experimental width is too narrow, the wings will not have the necessary surface area to spin and float back to you. Conversely, if the wings are too wide, the boomerang will curve upward and fall short of returning to you.

There are a few more things to consider here. With a shorter boomerang, the forward velocity of the boomerang will be slower because the distance from your wrist to the center of mass—where the wings cross—is shorter. More importantly, since the blades are shorter, they will have to spin faster to generate the necessary lift for a sharp return. This means that you will have to throw the shorter boomerangs harder and put more snap in your wrist to get them to return to you. However, once you hit the correct proportion of length to width, these boomerangs fly very well. You will find that a thinner, lighter paper is better for making the shorter paper boomerangs.

Longer Boomerangs: The 9-Inch, 10-Inch, and 11-Inch Paper Boomerangs

For these longer boomerangs, you should experiment with thicker varieties of paper. Rag paper, a rather expensive art paper at around $10 a sheet, is very smooth on both sides and comes in large sheets (see the 500 Series 4-ply bristol board from Strathmore, available at www.strathmoreartist.com). A less expensive option is to use a 0.024-inch rigid cover stock that is used by many printers. A paper of this thickness can be used for the 10-inch boomerangs. They fly extremely well, but the dynamics of their flights will differ slightly.

When increasing the length of the boomerang, even when you use a thicker paper, the wing will be floppier. This often adds extra elements of excitement, uncertainty, and surprise when trying to predict the flight path of a boomerang, especially when it is thrown a little too fast. It tends to veer when thrown in this way. But longer, indoor paper boomerangs are often beautiful and graceful in flight. The wings are wider, and the longer boomerangs, the ones made with Strathmore, fly in short, lazy circles that younger children really love.

Long, Thick, Rigid Outdoor Paper Boomerangs

Although this book is primarily about small, indoor paper boomerangs, larger paper boomerangs can be constructed and used outside. The thick, rigid paper needed for these boomerangs is very difficult to cut, so you will need a very good paper cutter with a long handle. A small paper cutter will work, but you have to apply more force to a cutter that has a shorter handle. You can fasten the wings with a heavy-duty stapler, such as the Swing-line 390 heavy-duty stapler. This stapler has a long arm for a greater amount of leverage.

For paper, you might try using Canson Mi-Teintes mat board. It comes in different colors and is often found in art supply stores. This thick board is usually cut to 16 by 20 inches. It is 0.061 inches thick and excellent for making outdoor boomerangs. For the size above, it costs between $2 and $3 a sheet. Crescent Hot Press illustration board is another thick, rigid paper. The wings work well at around 12 inches in length, but you may have to do a little experimentation here.

You may want to glue together two sheets of 0.021-inch railroad board. The boards must be aligned so that they both have the grain going in the same direction. This will make the paper 0.021 inches plus 0.021 inches, or 0.042 inches thick. This makes a very rigid board.

You may encounter a little problem here. If you cut your wings out of this board, they may be too thick and blunt. Boomerangs made in this way often work well, but the blunt edges may slow the rotation of the boomerangs too much. If this is a problem, do not cut the thick wings out of two large glued boards. Instead, glue the individual wings, but not directly on top of each other. Slide the two papers for a wing so that one strip sticks out about 0.04 to 0.08 inches beyond the other. This will make the leading and trailing edges half as much, or 0.021 inches. An adhesive spray can be used on large sheets, but a glue stick works fine on the individual strips. If you use adhesive spray on large sheets, you can use a rubber roller (brayer) to press the sheets together.

Boomerangs with thicker wings tend to fly in larger circles. Of course, if you want them to fly in very large circles, the wings should be thick and weighted with a heavy material. For example, if the wings of a thick-winged boomerang are weighted with foil, you will need an auditorium for flying it. Using foils is discussed in chapter 13. Also see the list of materials in the appendices at the back of this book.

A Final Note: The Importance of Experimentation

In the end, making and throwing paper boomerangs is an art that includes a bit of science and engineering. Experimentation is essential—you must observe their movement and modify their designs in order to achieve the most elegant flights possible.

When selecting and manipulating paper and other materials, there is one commandment: *know thy materials*. Gain a feeling for what they will do under different conditions. Mastering the boomerang is like playing a musical instrument. A boomerang's flight depends on how it is thrown, so a thrower must also be aware of the positions of the relevant parts of his or her own body to perfect his or her technique. With just a little patience and practice, you'll enjoy flying paper boomerangs and enjoy introducing them to others as well.

13

Action Shots
and
Final Notes

In making paper boomerangs, how they look is almost as important as how they are designed. Professional kite designers have known this for centuries. With outdoor boomerangs, colorful designs are now as much a part of modern boomerangs as the aerodynamic qualities of their wings. For a boomerang, a beautiful flight is in itself a joy to watch—especially when the return is sharp and fast—but a colorfully painted paper boomerang will enhance your enjoyment of the boomerang's flight.

The following photographs help to illustrate this point. Though they are not shown in color here, you can see the color photos on my Web site, www.paperboomerangs.com. The "fan" images you see were achieved by holding the camera's shutter open longer than usual. Though they appear to be moving quickly, the boomerangs in the photos below were actually spinning quite slowly. The stripes you see are made from different colors on the boomerangs' wings. When they spin fast enough, the stripes form circles of the same color. By varying the color, width, and placement of the stripe along the wing, you can create some surprising effects.

A spinning red, green, and white paper boomerang.

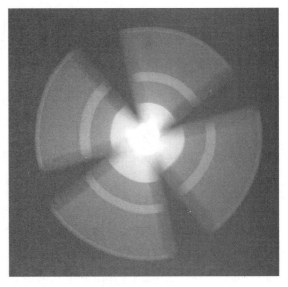

Spinning paper boomerang.

The photos below show the same boomerang spinning at two different speeds. The second boomerang is spinning faster than the first. When a boomerang spins quickly, your eye sees a similar circular image. This circle is created by a phenomenon called *persistence of vision*—a faint afterimage of an object remains on your eye's retina for approximately ½₅ of a second, causing the next thing you see to merge together with it. (This is why a motion picture, which is just a collection of still photographs flashing by at 24 images per second, appears to move.)

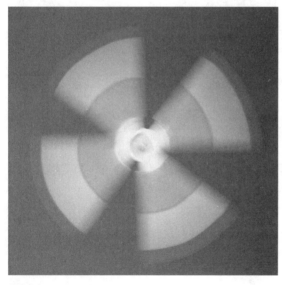

Spinning paper boomerang.

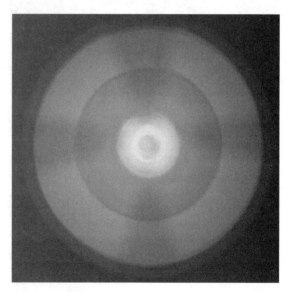

Spinning boomerang.

Experiment with different patterns on your boomerangs' wings, as seen in the images below.

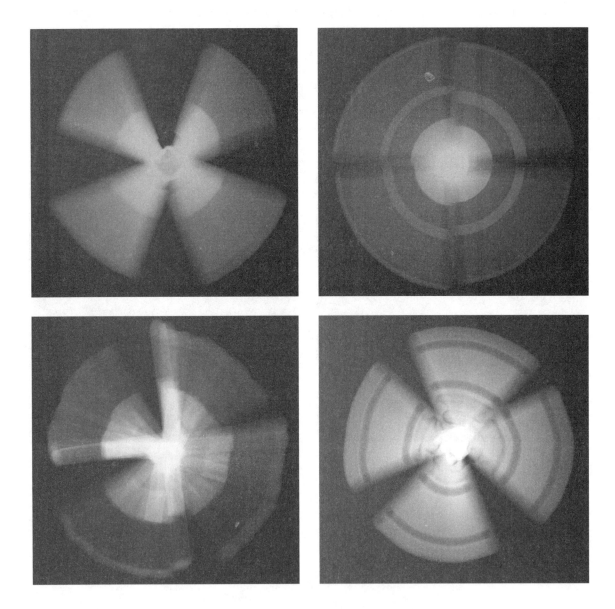

Again, the photos below show the same boomerang rotating at different angular velocities. Often, as the second photo shows, you will not be able to predict exactly what type of spinning image you will get from a particular colorful design. Sometimes the colors seem to grade into one another in unexpected ways.

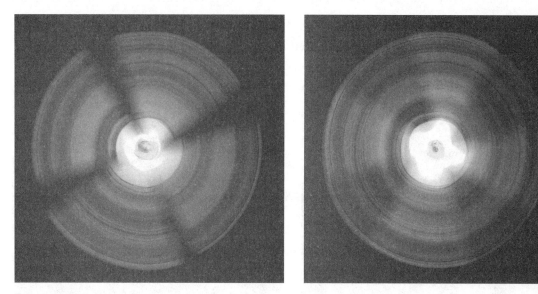

Two shots of the same boomerang.

Glow-in-the-Dark Boomerangs

Glow-in-the-dark boomerangs are a lot of fun. They can be made easily using photolumi-nescent tape. Curl the tape around the wing tips or place strips along the top and bottom of the wings. To charge the tape, place it near a bright light source for a few minutes, then turn out the lights and practice flying your boomerang in the dark.

The image on the right below was created by placing the tape as shown on the left.

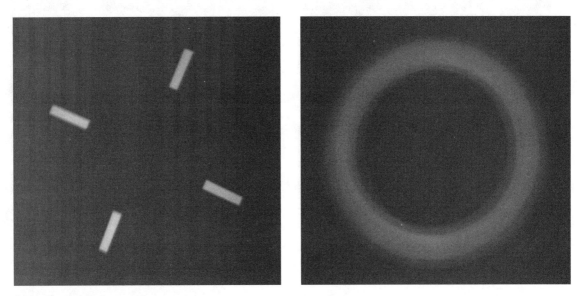

A glow-in-the-dark paper boomerang.

You can create even more complex patterns by placing pieces of tape in multiple positions along the wings. This will make for very impressive images in flight.

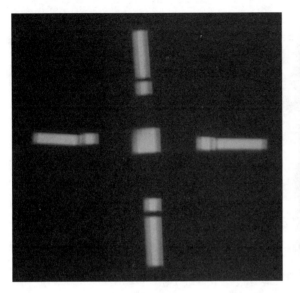 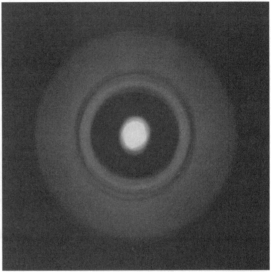

You can also use a photoluminescent paint on the wings as well. It works just as well as taped stripes do.

These glowing boomerangs are very easy to catch when you turn out the lights. As they fly, they will create large circles of green light.

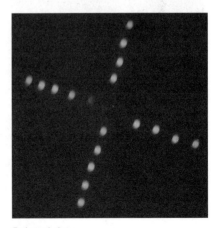

Painted dots.

Additional Materials

The photo below shows several of the materials I use to decorate my paper boomerangs.

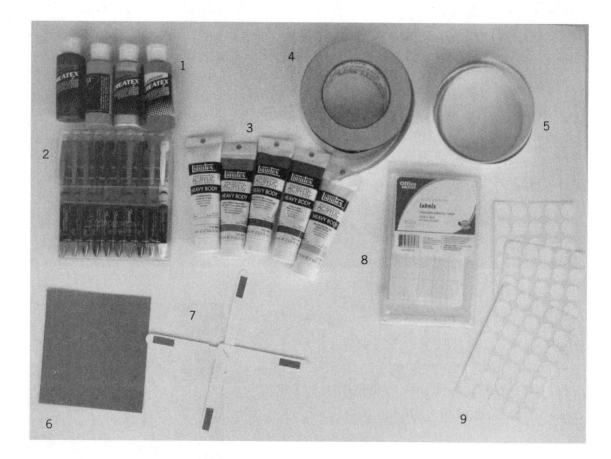

Item 1 is a series of fluorescent and iridescent airbrush colors by the paint manufacturer Createx. These are extremely bright and can be painted on the wings with a brush, roller, or air brush. If you plan to apply a lot of it, you will first have to prepare the paper with a coating to prevent the paper from absorbing water and curling. Each bottle comes with a cap that has a small opening that can be used to apply single drops of the paint to the wings. For a uniform coating, the edges of an 8-inch-by-11-inch piece of paper can be dipped into a small container and hung up to dry. The standard 8-inch-by-¾-inch wing strips can then be cut from the paper. The paint simultaneously adds weight to the wing tips and will increase the angular momentum of the spinning wings. Multiple coatings may be used to shape the surface of the wings, but you will have to experiment with this. Each individual wing may also be dipped in the paint.

Item 2 provides a convenient method to color the paper wings. These Sharpie Accent liquid highlighters are very bright and hold their color well. They can be purchased in a pack of 12 markers. Some other highlighter brands will not write on the cover-stock coatings made by some paper companies. The chemical reaction between the liquid of the highlighter and the coating of the paper also may produce a duller version of the color after it has dried on the wing.

Item 3, Liquitex acrylic paints, are water-based and can also be used when coating wings. The paint comes out thick and can be applied in successive layers to produce slightly different flight characteristics for a given paper wing. A fairly thick gob of it will dry overnight. The surfaced can be rippled if the paint is applied with a brush, but even though the surface is rippled, the ripples are smooth. This may allow you to experiment with texturing the wings in different ways.

Item 4 is silver Nashua metal foil tape. It is inexpensive, and one roll will probably last quite a while. Since the density of the metal foil is greater than paper's, it is an excellent way to weight the wing tips. It can be curled completely around the wing tips or applied as individual strips on the tops and bottoms of the wings. If you use the Strathmore 500 Series smooth plate paper, which is 0.024 inches thick, along with the metal foil, the paper boomerang will have to be flown in an auditorium or other large indoor space.

Item 5 is strip of 1-inch-wide phosphorescent (glow-in-the-dark) tape that can be found at www.ridesafer.com. A 5-foot strip costs $5. The tape is 0.015 inches thick and can be wrapped around the tips of a boomerang's wings.

Item 6 is an orange retroreflective sheet. The backing can be peeled off, and it can be applied to any smooth surface. This is the same kind of reflective material that stop signs are made of. It is composed of microglass beads that reflect light back toward the source at night. The boomerang in the photo (item 7) is weighted with this material. The sheet has a very smooth surface and is fairly heavy. A boomerang coated with this will have a very sharp and fast return.

Items 8 and 9 are more paper labels. Office Depot sells this pack of 1,000 white labels (⅝ by ⅞ inch). They are convenient to use for weighting the wings. The round green labels are also easy to place on the wings. The boomerang on the right has green tips, silver foil weights, and a striking fluorescent yellow-green area produced by the Sharpie Accent highlighter.

It may be possible to layer this foil and do a little wing shaping with it. This boomerang will

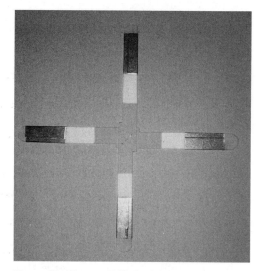

Heavy Strathmore 500 Series bristol board with metal foil.

go out about 45 feet. Here, the foil is wrapped around the wing tips, but it may also be layered on the tops and bottoms of the wings. With a little experimentation, varying the placement of the foil might give a more circular flight path.

Wrapping the foil around the wing alters the shape of the wings at those covered areas of the trailing and leading edges. Experiment with wrapping a thicker but narrower strip of foil at the wing tips. This will concentrate the weight farther from the axis of rotation and will affect less of the surface of the trailing and leading edges. There are many combinations that you can work through here.

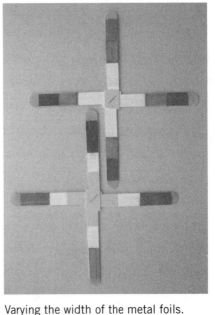

Varying the width of the metal foils.

The top boomerang in the photo at left has round green labels with fluorescent drops of Createx airbrush paint. Drops of paint can first be applied to the labels; the label with the drop can be attached to the wings later. The bottom boomerang has several wavy lines that form ridges. This is also a way to texture the wing surface to affect the characteristics of the flight.

The image on the photographic paper at the top of the next page was created in CorelDRAW, a graphics editing program, and printed with a standard ink-jet printer. The 1¾-inch-wide strips were glued to both sides of a

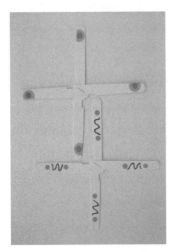

Using paint drops as weights.

0.020-inch-thick cover stock (Carolina, 8-inch-by-11-inch sheet) with a glue stick. This paper is produced by International Paper. As cover stock goes, it is relatively inexpensive. This particular boomerang has a very circular flight path. Surprisingly, it travels quite far out before returning.

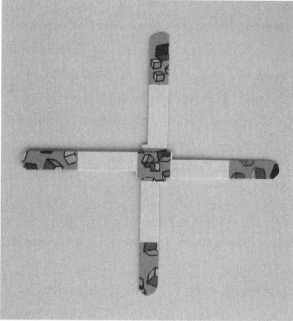

Weights of Epson 44-lb. premium presentation paper.

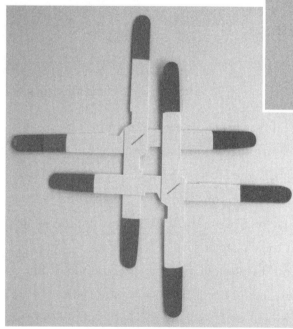

Wing tips dipped in bright fluorescent paint.

The boomerangs at left have brilliant red tips (except for one tip on the top left that is green). Dipping the tips forms a uniform color coating. Multiple dips can be done to increase the weight—and therefore the angular momentum—of the boomerang.

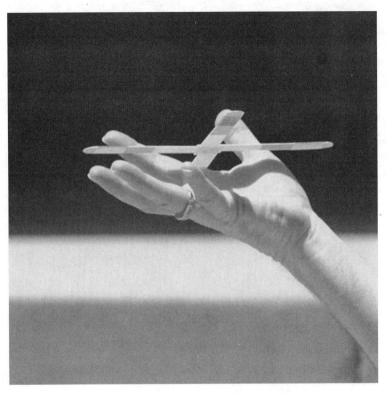

An easy catch.

Appendix A

Material Sources and Specifications

While the materials in list 1 and list 2 are recommended to build a thorough paper boomerang-making kit, you're encouraged to experiment with the materials found in list 3 as well.

List 1: The Minimum

1. Railroad board
2. Scissors (3½-inch cutting blades)
3. Yardstick
4. Glue stick
5. Pencil
6. Stapler

List 2: You Might Want to Add . . .

1. Small paper cutter (with a 15-inch cutting blade)
2. Origami paper
3. Highlighters (Sharpie Accent liquid highlighters)

List 3: For the Serious Hobbyist

1. Paints
2. Spray Mount Artist's Adhesive by 3M (for attaching strips of decorative paper)
3. Tapes and foils (metal and nonmetallic for decoration and weighting wings)
4. Three-inch rubber roller (brayer) for securing the decorative paper strips
5. Paintbrushes (for artists)
6. Labels
7. Adhesive putty
8. Photoluminescent tape (made by Identi-Tape, www.identi-tape.com)
9. Gyroscopes (just for fun)
10. Photographic paper
11. Mat boards (available from Canson, Crescent, and other manufacturers)
12. Dymo Office-Mate II

Wing Paper

Sources

Six-ply railroad board (0.021 inches thick, or 21 point) can usually be found at the following types of retailers: teacher's supply stores, arts and craft supply stores, and office supply stores. CAUTION: Some sales personnel at office supply stores use the terms "railroad board" and "poster board" synonymously. Poster board is usually thinner and will not work!

The following national chain stores carry railroad board: **Lakeshore Learning stores**, **Blick Art Materials**, and **Utrecht Art Supplies**. These particular businesses usually carry single sheets. They all have store locators online. Lakeshore Learning (www.lakeshorelearning.com) is one of the least expensive stores from which to buy this paper. They will also carry 100 sheet cases in assorted colors for about $56 per case.

Pacon Creative Products, a major supplier of railroad board, also has a store locator on its Web site. Go to www.pacon.com and then click "Where to Buy" at the top of the page. Put in your zip code and how far away from your home you're willing to travel, check the box for railroad board, and click "Search." But remember, even if the store locator says a particular store carries this paper, it may be out of it, so be sure to call first.

Railroad board can also often be found at **Office Depot** and sometimes **Staples**. Office Depot may have single sheets of this 6-ply board, but if they do not, you can order single-color packs of 25. These packs come in many colors, including magenta (item number 838290), emerald green (838059), red (838220), dark blue (838339), royal blue (838332), kelly green (838087), canary (838150), white (837975), and black (838374) and usually cost around $23 each, but the price varies according to color. Office Depot also has 100-sheet cases of assorted colors of the 22-inch-by-28-inch 6-ply railroad board (0.022 inches thick). It is $112.99 per case (item #355388).

Strathmore Artist Papers (www.strathmoreartist.com) is a division of Pacon Corporation. The Strathmore 500 Series 4-ply bristol board makes great paper boomerangs. Go to the company's Web site, click "Where to Buy" in the left-hand column, click "Retailer Locations," and select your state. For example, this site lists approximately 300 art supply stores in California that carry the company's products. Not all the stores have this product, so you should call the stores in your area before you visit them.

International Paper (www.internationalpaper.com) manufactures cover stock that makes wonderful paper boomerangs. Their Carolina C2S cover stock is an excellent paper to use. (Some small printers and die-cutting companies also use this cover stock and may have some on hand for you to experiment with.) International Paper is a huge company. They have many distributors, but the smallest quantity that distributors will sell is usually a carton of 300 sheets. If you want a large quantity, look for a local distributor. If you call International Paper, they will give you the name of a local distributor in your area (if there is one).

My Web site, **www.paperboomerangs.com**, also carries most of the papers mentioned in this book.

Specifications

- **Pacon Corporation railroad board:** 6-ply, 0.021 inches thick, 22-inch-by-28-inch sheets, single sheets for $1

- **Strathmore 500 Series bristol board:** 4-ply, 23-inch-by-29-inch sheets, smooth surface, $8–9 per sheet

- **International Paper Carolina C2S cover stock:** Coated on two sides, 0.020 inches thick, 23-inch-by-35-inch sheets, purchased in a carton of 300 sheets for about $160, base weight of 240 pounds, inexpensive if purchased in large quantities (stock code 008440)

- **Fabriano Artistico traditional white:** 22-inch-by-30-inch sheets, 300 pound, hot press, expensive
- **Canson mat board:** Extremely thick board, requires a sturdy paper cutter and heavy-duty stapler (make the leading edge cuts with a pair of scissors)
- **Crescent Hot Press illustration board:** Extremely thick, requires a sturdy paper cutter and heavy-duty stapler

Decorative Paper

Origami Paper

Would you like to make origami boomerangs? Origami paper can be found at craft stores and at online stores that specialize in this particular type of paper. There are some great online stores that carry it—just type "origami paper" into a search engine. You can also print your own.

The following companies also carry origami paper: **Paper Jade** (www.paperjade.com), **Origami Craft Supply** (www.origamicraftsupply.com), **Origami Corner** (www.origami corner.com), and **Creative Papers Online** (http://handmade-paper.us/), to name only a few.

Photographic Paper

Photographic paper is flat and does not leave fibers along the edge when it is cut. This type of paper also comes in different weights. If you are going to print your own designs using an ink-jet printer, I would recommend **Epson** matte 27-pound presentation paper (www.epson.com).

Nonpaper Items

The following items are only suggestions. I encourage you to experiment with various materials to perfect the look of your boomerangs and the quality of their flights.

- **Dymo Office-Mate II:** This label maker prints on vinyl strips that work extremely well as wing weights for lighter boomerangs. Although there are less expensive ways to attach wing weights (and you should use those methods before using this product), this instrument is very convenient and uses $\frac{3}{8}$-inch-wide strips of vinyl. The machine advances the strip about $\frac{1}{8}$ of an inch for each squeeze of the hand lever. This makes it easy to control the length (weight) of the strip. The device scores the backing of the vinyl so that it is easy to separate.
- **Labels:** I recommend the $\frac{1}{2}$-inch-by-$1\frac{3}{4}$ inch Avery Dennison Easy Peel white return address labels. Small round labels can also be used.
- **Paints:** Createx fluorescent and iridescent airbrush colors, Liquitex acrylic artist colors, and paint pens are only a few that you can try. You can also experiment with Scribbles 3D paint to color, weight, and shape the paper wings. This fluorescent paint comes in 1-ounce bottles.
- **Tapes and Foils:** There are many colorful vinyl, Mylar, and metal tapes. There are also colorful origami foils that can be purchased online. Nashua aluminum tape is not expensive and can be found at the Home Depot. It is a very soft aluminum tape and an excellent product for weighting the wings for long flights.
- **Staplers:** For stapling two 6-ply railroad board wings together (0.021 inches plus 0.021 inches), you will need a stapler that can staple 20 sheets of 20-pound paper.

Garrett Wade has a small, handheld stapler that is very convenient. It measures 4½ inches by 2½ inches by ¾ inch and costs about $13 (stock number 06T03.10). It will easily staple two railroad-board wings together. For stapling extra-thick stock, use something equivalent to the Swingline 390 heavy-duty stapler. It has ⅜-inch staples and will easily penetrate 0.082 inches of paper.

- **Gyroscopes:** Gyroscopes are a lot of fun. You don't need a gyroscope to make a boomerang, but for those interested in extending their understanding of gyroscopic behavior, the original Chandler toy gyroscope (1917 model) is still available online for $5 or $6. In addition, Gyroscope.com (www.gyroscope.com) carries many models, but the Super Precision Gyroscope, which comes with extensions for demonstrations and spins at 12,000 rpm, is very interesting. The purchase price with postage is about $100. Other, less expensive gyroscopes can be found at Edmund Scientific (http://scientificsonline.com) and Tedco Toys (www.tedcotoys.com). If you'd like to see a fantastic photo gallery of historic and unusual gyroscopes, see www.gyroscopes.org/gallery.asp.

Appendix B

The Best Boomerang Web Sites

These Web links and more—including links to online videos of boomerangs in flight—are available on my Web site, www.paperboomerangs.com.

Technical and Professional Boomerang Sites

Boomerang Association of Australia: www.boomerang.org.au

Boomerang Science: http://antoine.frostburg.edu/college/chemistry/senese/
chemed-l/199901/0064.html

Cleveland Boomerang School: www.clevelandboomerangschl.com

Flying Frog Boomerangs: www.angelfire.com/nc/conally/construction.html

Hyperphysics: http://hyperphysics.phy-astr.gsu.edu/hbase/brng.html

Leading Edge Boomerangs: www.leadingedgeboomerangs.com

Swiss Long-Distance Boomerangs: www.baggressive.com

United States Boomerang Association: www.usba.org

Where to Buy Boomerangs

Aerobie: www.aerobie.com

Australian Returning Boomerangs: www.returningboomerangs.com/index.htm

BambooRang: www.bamboorang.com

Blue Star Rangs: www.sports-boomerangs.com

Boomerang Fan: www.boomerangfan.com

Boomerang World: www.flight-toys.com/boomerangs.htm

Boomerangman: www.theboomerangman.com

Boomerangs.com: www.boomerangs.com

Broadbent Boomerangs: www.broadbentboomerangs.com

Colorado Boomerangs: www.coloradoboomerangs.com

Crescent Moon Boomerangs: www.crescentmoonboomerangs.com

Cryderman Boomerangs: www.worldsgreatboomerangs.com

Davro Boomerangs: www.davroboomerangs.com

Everything Australian: www.everythingaustralian.com/boomerangs.html

Forever Flying: www.foreverflying.com/boomerangs.html

Kendall Davis: www.kendalldavis.us

Rangs Boomerangs: www.rangsboomerangs.com

Glossary

Airfoil The cross-sectional shape of an airplane or boomerang wing that, when air flows over it, is designed to create a force called lift.

Angular velocity The rate of an object's spin.

Axis An imaginary line about which a body rotates.

Boundary layer The layer of air that is next to the surface of a wing.

Bowing The tendency of a paper wing to curve to one side or the other.

Brittleness A paper is brittle if it tears easily; also, when a paper sheet is bent, if the fibers within it break, then the paper is said to be brittle.

Crispness The property of a sheet of cover stock or railroad board that seems to add to the paper's stiffness while not making it overly brittle. Scissors feel a little different and make a slightly different sound when they cut a paper that has this property. It may be that the paper is a little harder. Most often it is a batch of black railroad board that will display an additional crispness.

Density The amount of matter in a given volume of space, or the amount of mass per unit of volume. Density equals mass divided by volume.

Drag The force that opposes the forward motion of a wing through the air.

Fiber Paper has fiber or small threads; if the fiber runs mostly in one direction across a sheet of paper, the sheet is said to have grain.

Grain This refers to the alignment of the fibers in paper. If the fibers run the length of a sheet of paper, the paper will have a greater resistance to being bent along its length. The grain must run along the length of a paper boomerang's wing for it to be rigid.

Laminar flow The smooth, layered, continuous flow of air around a wing.

LE The leading edge of a boomerang wing, the edge that is slicing through the air.

Lift The reactive force caused by the motion of air over an airfoil.

Mass The measure of an object's resistance to acceleration. The more mass an object has, the harder it is to move it. For most practical calculations here on Earth, mass is synonymous with weight.

Moment of inertia A spinning object's ability to resist changes in its rotation. If you hold a spinning gyroscope in your hand and try to rotate it in space, you will feel resistance to this motion caused by the gyroscope's high moment of inertia.

MTA Boomerangs specifically designed to stay aloft for a maximum time (maximum time aloft) are called MTAs.

Ply The layers in a paper product are called ply; a 6-ply paper has six layers.

Precess To fly in a circular path. A boomerang precesses and also spins on its axis.

Radius The length of a line extending from the center of a circle (or sphere) to its edge.

Ream A ream is usually 500 sheets of paper.

Rigidity The paper from which boomerangs are made must by stiff, or rigid. Rigidity depends on the direction of the grain in the paper and on the layering of the paper.

Side throw The side throw is the most common mistake when attempting to throw a paper boomerang.

Streamlines A collection of curves that illustrate the flow of air toward, over, and under a wing.

Surface roughness The degree of smoothness of a paper wing that helps determine the wing's drag; a rougher surface has more drag.

TE The trailing edge of a boomerang wing, on the opposite side of the wing from the LE, or leading edge. The TE does not cut through the air.

Torque A twisting force, such as the force created when certain parts of a boomerang are subjected to greater lift than others.

Volume The amount of space that an object takes up, expressed in cubic units.

Weight The force exerted on an object by gravity. For most practical calculations here on Earth, weight is synonymous with mass.

Wrist flick The quick forward movement of the wrist just prior to releasing the boomerang. It causes the boomerang to spin and float.